THE SKYCOURT AND SKYGARDEN
GREENING THE URBAN HABITAT
JASON POMEROY

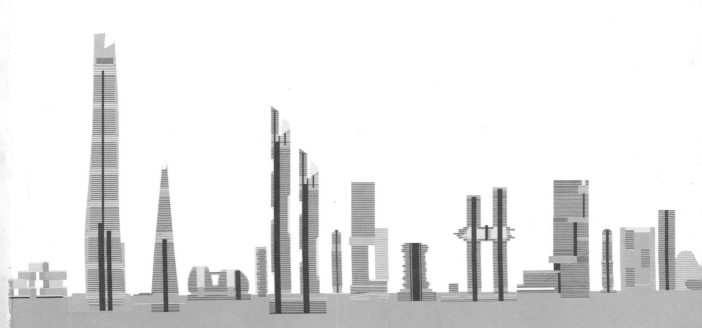

Routledge
Taylor & Francis Group

LONDON AND NEW YORK

First published 2014
by Routledge
2 Park Square, Milton Park, Abingdon, Oxon OX14 4RN

and by Routledge
711 Third Avenue, New York, NY 10017

Routledge is an imprint of the Taylor & Francis Group, an informa business

© 2014 Jason Pomeroy

British Library Cataloguing in Publication Data
A catalogue record for this book is available from the British Library

Library of Congress Cataloging Data
The skycourt and skygarden : greening the urban habitat / Jason Pomeroy.
    pages cm
    Includes bibliographical references and index.
    1. Public spaces. 2. Tall buildings--Social aspects. 3. Courtyards.
    4. Urban gardens. 5. Architecture--Human factors. I. Title.
    NA9053.S6P66 2013
    720'.4--dc23
    2013016828

ISBN: 978-0-415-63698-8 (hbk)
ISBN: 978-0-415-63699-5 (pbk)
ISBN: 978-1-315-88164-5 (ebk)

Designed and typeset in Catriel by Elizabeth Simonson

Printed and bound in India by Replika Press Pvt. Ltd.

To Yasmin

Contents

Foreword

Public spaces, such as the street and square, have provided for centuries a social platform that has supported society's day-to-day civic needs. It has been a means of 'transference', be that of material goods, knowledge, secrets, movement, culture, or spiritual or political message. Social change has however heightened the depletion of public space and accelerated its privatization, resulting in the consequent birth of alternative social spaces that started to wield more influence in the urban habitat. The semi-public realm, captured within hybrid structures, has developed through the centuries into a collection of new social spaces that possess some of the qualities that one would associate with successful public spaces – memorable places that embody character, a continuity of frontage or a sense of enclosure to create 'outdoor rooms', a well maintained and policed environment conducive to society's co-presence, an ease of movement, a legibility, an adaptability to changing social, political or economic need, and a diversity of use and function.

This book considers skycourts and skygardens in terms of the social, economic, environmental and spatial benefits that they provide to the urban habitat. The book argues that they have the potential to be 'alternative' social spaces that can form part of a broader multi-level open space infrastructure that seeks to replenish the loss of open space within the urban habitat. Both the skygarden and skycourt's incorporation into buildings can be viewed almost as a vertical rotation of Nolli's traditional figure ground plan, albeit to create a figure section. It starts to illustrate how semi-public spaces can be incorporated into high-rise structures, and be suitably placed into a hierarchy of open spaces that supports the primary figurative voids on the ground or, in their absence, creates them in the sky (diagram of vertical extrapolation). It also advocates for a new hybrid that can harness the social characteristics of the public domain, but placed within the figurative private object as an alternative social space for the 21st century.

This is an instructive publication that expands with greater elaboration the notion that tall buildings should be designed as 'vertical urban design', requiring the creation of 'public' places in the sky (Yeang, 2002). This challenges the often pre-conceived ideas of many skyscraper architects who continue to design and build tall buildings as a multiple stack of homogenous floor plates, one on top of the other. Whilst making construction structurally expedient and economically efficient for the engineers, it is the repetition of the typical floor plate over seemingly endless floors that gives the tall building its often negative reputation. Pomeroy's book considers skycourts and skygardens as 'in-between' spaces and in terms of their social, economic, environmental and spatial benefits that are so crucial to humanising the urban habitat. One might regard this as a futuristic book, but many ideas about enhancing and creating a vibrant and pleasurable life in the high-rise are implementable now. Architects, developers and academics of high-rise buildings within the urban habitat could learn much from this treatise.

Ken Yeang (Dr.) (2013)

Preface

The seed of this book started with my research at Cambridge University. The research covered the socio-spatial functions of skycourts and skygardens, and in particular how the increasing privatisation of the public realm necessitated a re-evaluation of open space infrastructure within the modern city. The thesis has led to continued research in my design firm which is based in Singapore — an environment that lends itself well to the subject matter given the city-state's high-density/high-rise nature. Singapore forms a notable precedent for many a developing global city that is seeking to green its urban habitat, as its spatial constraint of being an island, coupled with a predicted population growth from approximately 5 million people in 2011 to 6 million by 2020, has seen continued vertical urban densification. Increased density to house a transmigratory population, and the need to address the economic prospects of a financial services sector expansion, led to state-run urban renewal projects becoming inseparable from relocating the majority of the local population from the centre, to high-density residential blocks that bore similarities to Le Corbusier's vision for the modern city (Tremewan, 1994).

Despite this, the city-state has investigated alternative social spaces of interaction, and more recently embraced skycourts and skygardens as a means of offering spatial replenishment for socio-environmental benefit. According to Antony Wood of the Council on Tall Buildings and Urban Habitat, Singapore offers a glimpse of what could be 'the closest reality to an urban utopia that we have anywhere in the World today' (Wood, 2009). It therefore may come as little surprise that many of the case studies that we shall see in this book originate from Singapore and, along with other global case studies, form a body of projects that embrace skycourts and skygardens as part of a new urban vocabulary. This book seeks to balance the creative vigour of leading architects and designer's in their pursuit of the new hybrid structures that include open space within the object, with an academic rigour of reference points that demonstrates the skycourt and skygarden's place within the high-density urban habitat.

Part 1, entitled 'Civility, community and the decline of the public realm', provides the traditional context of the city as the forum of our civil interaction. It seeks to define what it means to be out 'in public', the meaning of the words 'civility' and 'community', and what constitutes 'public realm' before considering the elements that contributed to its decay. This leads us to consider the physical transformation of the urban habitat from a city dominated by spaces for social interaction and movement, to a city of objects as a response to changing socio-economic need. It also highlights the consequent and gradual depletion of urban greenery through the process of urbanisation. This allows us to explore the socio-environmental consequences of the loss of open space through densification – namely compromised opportunities for social interaction that can hinder the forging of 'community,' and the eradication of urban greenery that compromises bio-diversity and amplifies urban heat island effect. Part 1 closes by reviewing the birth of alternative social spaces that have been created in response to such changes in the urban habitat. It discusses how these new environments have the common characteristic of being semi-public spaces within the confines of private developments – thus providing an opportunity for society to use them – but are ultimately programmed spaces with particular social restrictions.

Part 2, entitled 'Defining the skycourt and skygarden', highlights how such environments have become part of an extended urban space vocabulary in response to increasing densification and society's need for alternative social spaces. It defines skycourts and skygardens as spaces of transition and destination, and draws parallels to the earlier precedents of the 18th century court and the 19th century arcade. It covers the measures being taken to counteract perceived density through legislation, before highlighting some of the socio-environmental benefits of their incorporation within buildings. Existing built examples from around the world are referenced to demonstrate the benefits of skycourts and skygardens that cover social issues (such as how skycourts can be community-orientated spaces), environmental issues (such as how they can help absorb noxious pollutants and counteract urban heat island effect by the incorporation of greenery), and economic issues (such as how they can generate income when used as observation decks).

Part 3, entitled 'Global case studies', seeks to document projects that incorporate skycourts and skygardens as an integral part of building design. These case studies include a brief write-up accompanied by imagery comprised of a combination of line drawing, graphics and photographs. Figure ground and figure section diagrams are generated for each development to demonstrate the relationship between building and open space. Photographs of the building in context, and more detailed photographs of the skycourt and its use, complete the case study. In total, 40 global case studies are taken from Europe, North America, the Middle East and Asia that are deliberately divided into four parts to demonstrate the evolution of the new hybrid structures, namely:

- completed projects (examples of skycourt buildings that are occupied)

- under construction (projects on site that are not yet occupied)

- on the drawing board (schemes that are in the process of design development)

- future vision (projects of students and academics of our future urban habitats).

Part 4, entitled 'Towards a vertical urban theory', puts forward 'prompts for thinking' to optimise the design of skycourts and skygardens in the future in a way that integrates such spaces into the broader fabric of the city. It considers the rooftops of existing buildings as further opportunities for densification, social interaction and urban farming that relates back to the new vertical city. This chapter concludes by considering the 'age of authenticity' and the increasing trend towards evidence-based design to forward the design of such spaces in a more objective way. This provides the opportunity to discuss the space syntax method as a mechanism for a predictive theory of mass movement through space and measures of urban greenery through the green plot ratio method, which collectively can help the creation of more conducive spaces that will help foster more successful vertical communities, and a greener urban habitat.

It is probably apt to conclude on what our studio calls the '3Ds' – the ability to 'Distil, Design and Disseminate'. If we consider these words in isolation, it allows us to distil the lessons from the past in order to design for the present, and to then be able to disseminate the knowledge for future generations. This book has certainly been true to such a process. I owe a note of thanks to John Worthington and Alan Short – individuals who instilled in me a line of inquiry of historical precedents in order to distil the essence of an idea for the betterment of the contemporary built environment. I owe many thanks to those who have designed for the present and future generations, and extend my deepest gratitude to the many architectural practices that allowed us to document their works in the case studies. I am finally thankful to my team who helped disseminate the information through the book itself – with special thanks going to Elizabeth Simonson, An Anh Nguyen, David Calder, Phil Oldfield and Chloe Li. Last, and certainly not least, to Ken Yeang, my mentor, who has also provided the starting point for so many green designers in the pursuit of sustainable tall building design within the urban habitat.

Jason Pomeroy (Prof.) (2013)

Civility, community and the decline of the public realm

1. Civility, community and the decline of the public realm

1.1 The public realm, civility and community

'Public realm', 'public sphere' and its various other permutations have become commonplace in our day-to-day language. It helps us imagine the social environment in which we can freely express ourselves as well as the spatial environment in which we can interact through meeting, trading, rallying, celebrating or simply moving through (Figure 1). The Romans understood the public realm to stand for everything formal and official, and it became synonymous with governance and state interests. According to the academic Richard Sennett, the public realm represented 'those bonds of association and mutual commitment which exist between people who are not joined together by ties of family or intimate association… the bond of a crowd, of a people, of a polity, rather than the bonds of family and friends' (Sennett, 1976).

The philosopher Jurgen Habermas posited the notion of a 'public sphere' that allowed a civil society to come together in debate on matters of public good. This was undertaken on a common, inclusive platform that disregarded personal status. 'In its clash with the arcane and bureaucratic practices of the absolutist state, the emergent bourgeoisie gradually replaced a public sphere in which the ruler's power was merely represented before the people, with a sphere in which state authority was publicly monitored through informed and critical discourse by the people' (Habermas, 1989).

According to the academic Peter G Rowe, the success of the public realm lies in its pluralistic nature that need not cater to the particular whims of either civil society or state, but embodies a transcendental quality that permits both entities to share space through a healthy territorial tension that in the same instance recognises a mutual acknowledgement of the other's existence. It is 'a concept based on the belief that it is along the politico-cultural division between civil society and the state that the urban architecture of the public realm is made best, especially when the reach of both spheres extends simultaneously up to a civilization's loftier aims and down to the needs and aspirations of its marginalized populations' (Rowe, 1997).

Centuries have since passed, and despite an evolution in the way we interact and bond with fellow citizens, the idea of being civil in public remains. The day-to-day assertion

Figure 1: The street and square as a forum for demonstrating public opinion: a political rally in *Syntagma Square*, Athens

of a bond between people can be described as *civility* – a code of conduct that protects the individual in the public realm from unnecessary disclosures of personality, that could be detrimental to others as well as the individual. Sennett defines civility as a mask that permits sociability and interaction with others through detachment, and can act as a shield to private feeling. It can be formal, courteous and almost ceremonial in a manner that can mark the bond of a society. In the past, maintaining the mask of civility meant that public acts of expression were conscious decisions to maintain a distance and not reveal the true nature of one's private feelings. Such codes of conduct and agreements in a civil society have helped shape the urban environment in which we live today (Sennett, 1976).

The street and square have traditionally formed the built manifestation of the public realm and the focus of civil society's cultural formation, political practice and social encounter. Predominantly owned, governed and managed by the state, they have provided an environment for citizens to socially engage without fear of revealing one's character, and are born out of the necessary tensions between public (state) and private (civil society) to convert *space* into *place*. The street and square are the stage set for the theatre that is civil society's and state's social interaction. The square enables a diversity of spontaneous social and cultural experiences to take place – a multiplicity of use that can adapt according to shifting patterns in society, economy and political viewpoint. Squares are 'microcosms of urban life, offering excitement and repose, markets and public ceremonies, a place to meet friends and watch the world go by. They have been shaped by popular whims, by topography and architectural fashion' (Webb, 1990) (Figure 2).

Arguably, a public realm that provides an opportunity for the convergence of civil society and state interests similarly provides a forum for communities to appropriate such spaces. *Community* can be defined as a group of people living in the same locality or having the same religion, race, profession or interests. Academics David McMillan and David Chavis associate the sense of community with having boundaries, emotional safety, a sense of belonging and identification, personal investment and a common symbolic system (McMillan and Chavis, 1986). Various written

Figure 2: The square as a stage set for civil society's and state's social interaction: *Piazza San Marco*, Venice

permutations invariably reference the built environment ('commune', 'community centre', 'community home'), which is particularly telling of the intrinsic relationship between social groupings and the space or building needed to foster a sense of community, be that the piazza, mosque, office, clubhouse or café. These environments provide opportunities for like-minded individuals with similar interests to engage with one another, thus fostering a sense of community and identity through casual transaction and co-presence. Community also need not be fettered by geographical location, as we see in the virtual communities of the 'chat room', 'Facebook', or 'transpatial communities' [1] that are independent of place and are part of the individual's commitment to an institution, group or association.

The *Campo* in Siena is an example of an environment that draws upon such characteristics of a public space and has adapted through the centuries according to shifting social, political and cultural dimensions in order to continually redefine itself as a civic, memorable place (Figure 3). Its success owes much to a design that does not pander to the whims of civil society or satisfy grandiose gestures normally associated with state spaces. Instead, it is a place that addresses the sensitivities of different groups within society in its use and meaning, and shows no bias or marginalisation. Such neutrality allows the Campo to retain a multiplicity of function. It was an open-air church where clergy would give sermons as well as a political forum and a place of ceremony. It served as a regular market place and a destination for social interaction. It was also a venue for many of the Sienese traditional sports, such as the *Pugna* [2], or the *Palio* [3]. Such flexibility necessitated a system of control amongst the three predominant groups within the city: the government officials and bureaucrats; the civil society (made up of the nobility and the privileged); and the remaining middle and working classes who formed the citizens of Siena. This tri-partite arrangement was dynamic and fluid – as governments came and went, the fortunes of prominent families' waxed and waned and local neighbourhood associations varied in power and prominence (Rowe, 1997). Despite the sense of flux, there was an overall continuity born out of the strong relationship between civil society and state, and the belief that both were interdependent on the other that in turn created a sense of collective identity.

Figure 3: The square as a symbol of collective identity: *The Campo*, Siena

(1) Transpatial communities – a relationship independent of space. e.g. the membership of a Club, or clan, or visiting lecturing post to a university.
(2) The *Pugna* was an organised fight between rival neighbourhoods whereby one group attempted to push the other group out of the square.
(3) The *Palio* was a famous horse race that ran from point to point through the city streets of Siena and dates to the medieval ages.

Figure 4: The square as a place that marries state ambition with national unity: *Barcelona Urban Projects Programme*

The marriage of civil society and state to create a successful public realm can also be found in a contemporary example – the *Barcelona Urban Projects Programme* (Figure 4). From the end of the Spanish Civil War until his death in 1975, Francisco Franco's predominantly fascist dictatorship presented a dichotomy between itself and Spain's economic, social and cultural transformation, which was essentially a western European-influenced democratisation fostered through a burgeoning foreign investment programme and a liberal academic scene (Rowe, 1997). During Franco's regime, the Catalan region was deprived of support and any form of regional cultural expression was discouraged. Understandably, the period of democracy that followed saw the resurgence of Catalan regional identity, and the new political entities that were formed post-Franco created a counterbalance to the nationalistic resurgence. 'Thus in a fashion analogous to controversies surrounding the open space projects, a tension exists between a sense of unity (belonging to Spain) and a sense of being somehow separate and unique (being from Catalunya)' (Rowe, 1997). The result was a healthy tension between state and civil society, which would aid Barcelona's Urban Projects Programme. It would go on to demonstrate a commitment to diversity in the social arrangement and expression of the projects locally, often driven by the aspirations of various groups within civil society. The outcome was a series of public spaces that satisfied the state's ambition for a sense of national unity (between Catalunya and Spain) and the aspirations of the Catalans in reinforcing their own cultural identity in post-Franco Spain.

Both of these historical and contemporary examples demonstrate their capacity as settings for political, cultural and social life and reflect the enduring relationships between civil society and state. In doing so, they instil into the Sienese and the Catalunyan respectively a sense of place, of belonging, of identity and of civic consciousness. Yet the traditional public realm of the street and the square has increasingly come under pressure by both physical and ephemeral constructs of Man, and requires us to consider the social cause and effect in order for us to understand the spatial implications within the urban habitat.

1.2 The decline of the public realm, and the privatisation of space

Secularism, industrial capitalism, population increase and technological advances have been cited as the major contributors to the decline of the public realm and the consequent privatisation of space (Sennett, 1976; Hall, 2002; Lozano, 1990; Kohn, 2004; Madanipour, 2009). According to Sennett, the slow disintegration of the public realm can be partly attributed to the rise of secularism (Sennett, 1976). He has argued that understanding one's personality and emotion through the advent of modern psychology became more important than transcendental beliefs, which in turn fuelled the pursuit of fact and reason to explain the intangible or unknown. People's appearances and actions could thus be studied and understood, revealing the person behind the mask of civility. The public realm became a place where personal disclosure and the freedom to express one's personality become increasingly acceptable – a place where others could view private, personal displays of emotion and feeling as experiences. In doing so, the public realm became polarised – citizens comfortable with displays of personality and emotion became actors; citizens uncomfortable with such displays for fear of unnecessary disclosures of personality became spectators. Sennett has argued that society's increasing fixation with trying to understand one's personality by reading physical displays of dress and behaviour saw individuals withdraw in silence to seek solace in the family home in order not to betray their emotions in public. The fear of unveiling the mask of civility by revealing one's true personality, or even experiencing other people's revelations, thus contributed to the decline in the public realm, as individuals in society retreated to the comfort and security of their private domains (Sennett, 1976).

The places where personal interactions could took place, such as between the market trader and citizen in the sale and purchase of goods within the market square, were similarly challenged by another contributing factor: industrial capitalism (Sennett, 1976). The process of sale not surprisingly conformed to a similar code of civility, where public shows of emotion were still in fact masks. Outwardly, market traders could express emotions of indifference at a particular transaction that may well have concealed emotions of contentment from profit. The advent of new industrial methods of production, improved accounting, credit and investment methods, and the expansion of the cash

Figure 5: *The Spice Bazaar*, Istanbul: the market trader and citizen

economy, saw the rationalisation of business processes, which became increasingly impersonal. The introduction of mechanised means of production allowed goods to be produced quicker and cheaper, thus increasing productivity. Fixed prices negated the need to haggle, allowing for quicker sales and increased turnover. The growing profit margins through mass production inevitably saw the decline in market trading and its associated traditions, and consequently curtailed the activity within the public realm of the square. Society's investment in personality and consumer goods of mass production arguably had social repercussions in the individual's increasing withdrawal from the public sphere of interaction. It had also spatial repercussions in the pursuit of alternative social spaces to allow for social co-presence amongst the burgeoning bourgeoisie, as we shall see later.

Population increase and the consequent densification of cities had a further impact on our interactions in public. Le Corbusier's cure of clearing the slums and disease that lay behind the Haussmann façades of Paris sought to paradoxically decongest the city centre by increasing the density through modern high-rise structures. These buildings would contain 'perfect human cells which correspond[ed] most perfectly to our physiological and sentimental needs' whilst allowing the automobile to take precedence over the pedestrian (Hall, 2002) (Figure 6). The likes of Le Corbusier greatly influenced a post-war generation of qualifying architects both in Europe and around the world, spawning a legacy of high-density development that borrowed heavily from his concepts in order to address slum clearance, increasing land prices and an increasing birth rate that would lead to overcrowding. 'The big cities, many of which were not averse to keeping their own people rather than exporting them to new and expanded towns, read all this as a signal to build dense and build high' (Hall, 2002). The ability to re-house the masses into sanitised, high-density environments with (in the best case) supporting communal facilities, owed much to the early vision of Le Corbusier, but at the same time signalled the death of public spaces. This brought into increasing scrutiny how the new social spaces of the indoor street and outdoor raised plaza were to be used by the community. Social groupings and complete neighbourhoods, accustomed to low-rise urban environments with public space that permitted

Figure 6: *Plan Voisin*, Paris: Le Corbusier's answer to slum clearance and urban densification in Paris

casual interaction, were being dismantled and relocated into high-rise urban environments. The very same groups who once gathered to do their laundry, share in common activities or simply play in the streets were finding that the very spatial mechanisms that permitted communal activity and spontaneous chance meetings with neighbours were being socially and spatially engineered.

Urbanist Eduardo Lozano argues that technological advancement has further contributed to the 'break-up of urban life and community ... much human contact, which used to take place in streets, plazas and parks, has become packaged; romance has been replaced by singles bars or computer dating agencies' (Lozano, 1990) (Figure 7). Lozano asserts that the decline of the public realm has been compromised by technological advancement, and that there has been a disjuncture between the professional practice of creating architecture and the traditional cultural practice of building human habitats by the very community that live, work and play within them. We see this in the increasing dependency on energy-consuming artificial light and air conditioning that changes our living and working patterns, and further increases the disconnection from the rich milieu of open space and greenery that permits people to forge a sense of community through co-presence in public. The virtual realm further reduces the need to interact publicly, as one can be connected with an individual, group or association from the remotest parts of the world from the comfort of a laptop in the private domain of a dwelling, or office, alike. Books, magazines, television and music further reduce the need for those public places of encounter within the city, as public culture and collective belonging is achieved remotely.

Figure 7: Virtual space: a forum for engagement that negates the need for physical human contact through the use of technology

Such factors have thus contributed to the increasing privatisation of space, whereby the public domain is ceded to private interests who take control. The academic Margaret Kohn has considered the privatisation of space as a process of commodification, which occurs when 'something is turned into an object that can be bought and sold'. In her book *Brave New Neighborhoods*, Kohn defines the environments that embody public and private domain characteristics as social space – 'places that bring people together for the purpose of consumption' (Kohn, 2004). She argues that social space is a privatised construct in which people are encouraged to congregate and interact as if in public, though it has limitations and regulations on speech and action. For instance, social space exclusion of certain members of society and their activities can lead to segregation and, by implication, further erosion of democratic rights and processes that compromise spontaneity and life experiences (Kohn, 2004) (Figure 8).

The academic Ali Madanipour has similarly explored the commodification of space and in particular how real estate market forces promote the socio-spatial segregation of income groups and social classes. This 'has led to different patterns of access to space and hence a differential spatial organisation and townscape. Wherever there has been a tendency to de-commodify space, as in the post-war social housing schemes, townplanners and designers have ensured that a degree of spatial subdivision still prevailed' (Madanipour *et al.*, 1998). This creates differential access to the commodity (space), and furthermore relies on planning processes and design to regulate and control space production which can lead to 'collectivisation of difference, or exclusion, lead[ing] to enclaves for the rich and the creation of new ghettos for the poor' (Madanipour *et al.*, 1998).

Real estate market forces have similarly introduced greater urban responsibilities to be ceded to private development companies in the planning of developments. This further compounds the privatisation of spaces in order to ensure investment value may be maximised, and maintenance costs minimised, to preserve private interests. The resultant managed spaces, operated by private companies, may respond to market pressures by combating crime and vandalism, and by providing clean and well-maintained environments to meet consumers' expectations. But they may lack the spontaneity, accessibility and freedom of passage that can promote social inclusion that are generally associated with public spaces (Madanipour *et al.*, 1998). The gradual erosion of public spaces and the increasing privatisation of space therefore raises concerns of how such 'social spaces' are regulated, and whether speech and actions are controlled in a manner associated with private spaces. It also allows us to consider the spatial consequence of social change, and in particular the transformation from

Figure 8: The retail mall: a privatised space that embodies public domain characteristics

1.3 From a city of spaces to a city of objects

The architect Giuseppe Nolli's plan of Rome in 1748 revolutionised the way we graphically represent cities. The idea of being able to *poche*, or to blacken out the private buildings as a graphically solid form, reveals the distinctively open and public nature of the street, square and the civic institutional buildings. The practice that has become universally known as the *figure ground* plan establishes a hierarchy of space in relation to adjacent solids and voids. This need not be confined to the realms of urbanism, but is scalable to assist in the legibility of interior/exterior spatial relationships. When we look at the figure ground diagrams from the 18th century to present day, what is evident is the slow eradication of the figurative public space in lieu of the private object – particularly apparent in the graphical shift from white (representing space) to black (representing object) (Figure 9).

Changes in the way that civil society interacted – be that due to the effects of secularism, industrial capitalism, population increase, technological advancement or a combination of these factors – had a consequent spatial impact on cities. Such factors, and increasingly complex social codes of conduct, meant the city of spaces needed to adopt alternative spaces to cater for social, economic and technological change. By the middle of the 18th century, 'public space was implicitly traded for the private object; a deal that formally represented the beginning of the end of the *res publica*' (Dennis, 1986). Up until the 18th century, the city of spaces was determined from the outside in. The rationalised voids of the boulevard, street and square, acted as outdoor rooms that dictated city planning and provided a means of planned social interaction or chance meeting, trade and commerce, political activity, religious or cultural event. Meanwhile, the buildings' solid form accommodated the urban idiosyncrasies by acting as infill elements. Such a celebration of public life through the stage set of the square reaffirmed the predominance of (public) space over (private) object.

By the middle of the 18th century, however, the need for more housing, improved public utilities and transport infrastructure determined the city of spaces from the inside out. Rationalised solids of structural cores and service installations within the building started to dictate planning. Void spaces became the habitable space left over, and the free-standing private object

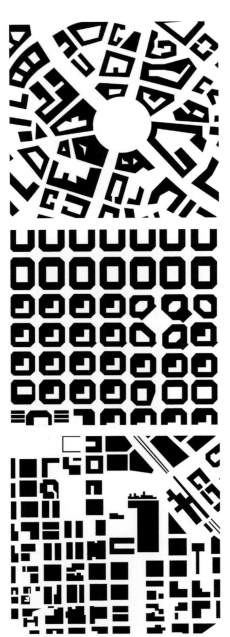

Figure 9 (top–bottom): Figure ground diagrams of 18th century Rome, 19th century Barcelona, and 20th century Portland

saw the public realm go further into decline. By the 20th century, the transformation was complete. The free-standing private object building sat within open, undifferentiated space that became the means of absorbing the urban idiosyncrasies. The modern city of objects represented the antithesis of the traditional city and heralded the predominance of object over space and the erosion of a public realm (Rowe and Koetter, 1978). Such a physical transformation is lucidly summarised by urbanist Colin Rowe and Fred Koetter's description of the diametrically opposite figure ground diagrams of the traditional and modern city: 'one is almost all white, the other almost all black; the one an accumulation of voids in largely unmanipulated solid; and, in both cases, the fundamental ground promotes an entirely different category of figure – in the one – object, in the other – space' (Rowe and Koetter, 1978).

Figure 10: *Petronas Twin Towers*, Kuala Lumpur: a symbol of a country's economic growth

The shift from an age of industry to an age of technology has seen the tall building within the city of objects become an alluring product of speculation – driven by the consequence of increasing land prices and therefore optimisation of land use to yield more favourable economic results. They have also become a means of demonstrating an individual's, a company's or a city's power and prestige amongst one's peers (Sudjic, 2005) (Figure 10). If we look at the construction of tall buildings from the 1920s to present day, we see that Man's desire to reach for the skies continues, with more and more audacious attempts to build the tallest peaking the curiosity of the media, developers and their respective cities and countries alike (CTBUH, 2012). According to the Council on Tall Buildings and Urban Habitat (CTBUH), we are likely to witness not only the world's first kilometre-tall building in this decade, but also the completion of a significant number of buildings over 600 metres (around 2,000 feet). This would place such a structure at twice the height of the *Eiffel Tower*. In 2009, prior to the completion of the *Burj Khalifa*, buildings of such a height did not exist. Yet by 2020, at least eight such buildings will exist internationally. The term 'supertall' (which refers to a building over 300 metres) is thus no longer adequate to describe these buildings, and instead we have entered the era of the 'megatall'. This has become a term officially used by the CTBUH to describe buildings now over 600 metres in height (CTBUH, 2011).

Tall buildings are not only defined by their height, but are increasingly being considered in light of their environmental responsiveness, given the increasing sensitivities of climate change and the typology's resource-intensive nature (Roaf, 2010). The academics Dario Trabucco and Phillip Oldfield have defined the tall building typology in five energy generations. These included the zoning laws of 1916, which set out rules on building proportion and 'set-back' in order to improve natural light and ventilation provision to the street. This was followed by the shift away from load-bearing masonry, to the advent of curtain walling during the 1930s. The development of more energy-efficient curtain walling systems as a response to the energy crisis of the 1970s was then followed by an awakened sense of environmentalism in the 1990s and a greater consideration of passive and active ventilation systems in tall buildings (Oldfield et al., 2008). In the new millennium, we also see the increasing influence of computer software in the generation of form in order to visually conceive on screen what one may not be able to draw on paper. The academic Karel Vollers has sought to catalogue twisting tall building forms (Vollers, 2009) – an exercise that re-affirms the popular paradigm shift away from the plate stacking exercise of what the academic Charles Jencks calls self-same repetition of the generic extruded tower, to self-similar structures that offer repetition in structure and envelope, and yet a dynamic and constantly changing form (Jencks, 2002) (Figure 11).

Figure 11: *30 St Mary's Axe*, London: challenging the 'self-same' tall building form by applying a 'self-similar' approach

The tall building is also no longer the reserve of just the office or residential typology. What was once a building typology that would be assigned to a singular function is increasingly embracing a vertical mixed-use programme of multiple-stacked components that assimilate compact city characteristics. The compact city, a dense microcosm of urbanity that optimises the density of various land uses and is integrated within an efficient transport infrastructure, has been heralded by the Organisation for Economic Co-operation and Development (OECD) as a preferred means of sustainable development (OECD, 2012). This is largely because of the compact city's capacity to preserve existing greenfield sites, and negate decentralised urban sprawl that would have been otherwise energy- and resource-intensive as well as heavily reliant on an expanded transport infrastructure. Its vertical reinterpretation in the mixed-use tower arguably 'future-proofs' against rising land prices through depletion of space in city centres and sector-specific downturns in the real estate economy (Watts, 2010). In 2011, 30% of tall buildings of over 200 metres were of the mixed-use (24%) or hotel (6%) function – a third of the total number of tall buildings built (CTBUH, 2012).

With extraordinary tall buildings being partly the result of a region's economic progress, it is unsurprising to note how the tall building has since developed in areas outside the historical tall building epicentre of the United States. In 2011, Central America, North America and Europe collectively completed 22% of the world's tall buildings that stand at 200 metres and above. Asia, however, completed the majority, with 48% (CTBUH, 2012). The shift in economic polarity from the developed West to a developing East can be seen in the physical manifestation of cities such as Jakarta, Manila and Kuala Lumpur that have flourished and seen their urban densities increase in a fashion not dissimilar to the development of Tokyo, Hong Kong and Singapore previously (Figure 12). In the context of the Asian city, density has often materialised in the form of the tall building typology, which has commonly been perceived as the panacea to spatial shortage and urbanisation. However, the research of Sir Leslie Martin *et al.*, has demonstrated that there are alternative (and more economic) means of achieving higher densities, not least the exploration of low- to medium-rise high-density typologies such as the courtyard or the terrace (Martin *et al.*, 1972). The consequence of planning for a city of objects is an attitude that runs the risk of denying the important role that space plays within the urban habitat, and requires consideration of the implications of open space depletion.

Figure 12: The Hong Kong skyline: tall buildings marking the rocky island's economic prosperity

1.4 Loss of open space, and its socio-environmental implications

The predominance of the city of objects over the city of spaces has, whilst permitting a range of new technologies to be explored, contributed to an increasing depletion of public space. Steel construction, the elevator, the air-conditioning system and the light bulb have all served Man to build taller and deeper floor plates. This has ameliorated the need to rely on masonry for load bearing, staircases for vertical means of access, or windows for fresh air and illumination. Dependence on such operational or embodied-energy -intensive elements within buildings has become the norm and almost inseparable from our day-to-day activities in much of the developed world. Paradoxically, such reliance not only has economic implications in the construction and running costs of tall buildings, but can also have detrimental health and well-being implications for its occupants.

Research has demonstrated that stress, boredom, restlessness and other psychological conditions have often been associated with the poor design of the high-density built environment as a result of 'directly or indirectly block[ing] important goals of users and also because the design may limit coping strategies for resolving the blockage' (Zimrig, 1983). Such goals of users often include the need to form bonds of association, intimate interaction and the ability to control the time and place for social co-presence to take place. When the environment does not support such psycho-social needs, social networks break down and may result in crime and vandalism at the public level (Figure 13); and withdrawal, depression and illness at a private level (Zimrig, 1983). Further environmental stress triggers include residential overcrowding and loud exterior noise sources, which can elevate psychological distress. Malodorous air pollutants within the city confines heighten the negative effect, and some toxins can also cause behavioural disturbances that can include aggression and the inability to self-regulate. Insufficient daylight is also reliably associated with increased depressive symptoms (Evans, 2003).

Figure 13: Environmental stress can elevate psychological distress and find expression in a variety of ways

Research has also shown that the absence of natural light, natural ventilation and a disconnection to the outside world can potentially lead to physiological conditions and building-related illnesses, such as Sick Building Syndrome (SBS) (Burge, 2004; Ryan and Morrow, 1992, Redlich *et al.*, 1997). SBS is manifested in symptoms related to the eyes, nose, throat and dry skin, along with more general symptoms of headaches and lethargy. Despite the discomfort and often debilitating capacity of SBS, the temporal relation with working in a particular building can improve within a few hours of leaving the vicinity. Whilst a building may be compliant to design standards, SBS may still occur and have a higher prevalence amongst occupants within air-conditioned buildings than naturally ventilated buildings. Other building attributes that have been associated with SBS include high indoor temperature (over 23°C in air conditioned buildings), low fresh-air ventilation in air-conditioned offices (<10 litres/sec/person), poor individual control of temperature and lighting, poor building service maintenance, poor cleaning and water damage (Burge, 2004).

The tall building typology within the city of objects has historically been perceived to exacerbate such psychological and psycho-social issues through the absence of open space and its most basic attributes of being able to provide natural light, ventilation and a congenial forum for social interaction. In the worst case, many high-rise, high-density developers and authorities failed to understand the importance of such open spaces being used to improve amenity, well-being, good health, productivity and social interaction, and were often omitted for economic reasons. Whilst JG Ballard's novel *High Rise* (2003) highlighted the potential for developments to be poorly conceived enclaves that were divorced from their surrounding context and crudely executed by local authorities, the social and physical disjunctures were all too clear to see in the reality of high-density estates such as *Pruitt Igoe*, Illinois (Figure 14). Here, a multitude of ills resulted in its eventual abandonment and its subsequent demolition. Drastic cost cutting and poor design, coupled with a local authority relocation programme of welfare families into the blocks, resulted in the Pruitt Igoe apartments and communal spaces falling into decline (Hall, 2002). The situation was compounded by a lack of understanding of how both the internal and external spaces would be used by the end-user. The resulting vandalism and deterioration thus created ghetto-like, indefensible spaces in and between the buildings. As noted by Oscar Newman, 'the architect was concerned with each building as a complete, separate, and formal entity, exclusive of any consideration of the functional use of grounds or the relationship of a building

Figure 14: *Pruitt Igoe*, Illinois: social and physical disjunctures resulted in vandalism and its eventual demolition

to the ground area it might share with other buildings. It is almost as if the architect assumed the role of sculptor and saw the grounds of the project as nothing more than a surface on which he was endeavouring to arrange a whole series of vertical elements into a compositionally pleasing whole' (Newman, 1980).

Environmentally, the proliferation of tall buildings within dense urban centres has contributed to the increase in urban temperatures (Wong and Chen 2006). Increase in urban temperatures can be further attributed to anthropogenic sources, including the heat released by air-conditioning plants, automobiles, artificial hard surfaces such as roads, pavements and façades; heat stored and released by complex high thermal mass urban structures; or a decrease in surface moisture that could otherwise cool the immediate environment through evapo-transpiration (Rizwan *et al.*, 2008). Studies have also shown that the high-rise, high thermal mass building typology further magnifies the impact on the urban climate, causing urban heat island effect (UHI) (Figure 15). This can be defined as the difference in temperature between the rural and urban areas (Arnfield *et al.*, 1999; Wong, 2010). The negative impacts of replacing open space and its landscape with building structures include increased health risks through higher ambient temperatures, aggravated atmospheric pollution, increased emissions of ozone precursors and increased energy consumption for cooling in the magnitude of 5% for every 1 degree of ambient temperature rise (Wong *et al.*, 2003).

Figure 15: Urban heat island: can be exacerbated by the reduction of urban greenery

Variance in the urban heat island has also been found to correlate to different land uses. In the case of Singapore, its urban morphology is made up of an array of object-driven configurations ranging from tall to medium to low-rise developments. Commercial, industrial and residential land uses characterise the island, with a predominance of residential blocks at the peripheries set within verdant landscape, a nature reserve to the north, industrial warehouses and business parks to the west and a centrally located business district defined by tall buildings. Studies have shown that the industrial/business parks to the west and the central business district have the highest urban heat island intensities, followed by the residential areas and the park area in descending temperatures (Jusuf *et al.*, 2007).

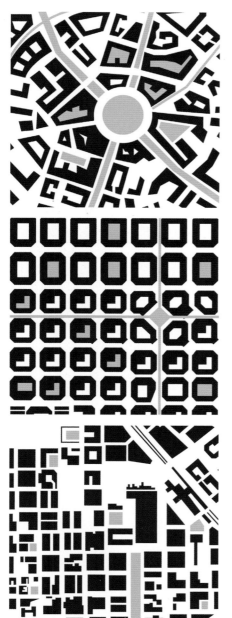

Figure 16: Depletion of open space can also suggest depletion of urban greenery

This suggests that the inclusion of greenery helps reduce the ambient temperatures, and is also testimony to the vital role space, and in particular landscaped open space, plays within our urban habitat.

What the figure ground diagrams from the 18th century to the present day graphically demonstrate is not just the slow eradication of figurative public space in lieu of the private object, but with it, the reduction in urban greenery (Figure 16). Despite the debilitating consequences of high-density tall building developments of the past, academics and built environment professionals alike acknowledge that spatial constraints, as well as the notion of power, prestige and the identity of cities, will continue to fuel Man's desire to build tall buildings. Nevertheless, the very same groups are increasingly seeking to consider more sustainable tall building solutions that can reduce energy consumption whilst fostering a sense of community and together enhance the built environment.

The reintegration of open space within the urban habitat and the tall building typology, in a fashion not too dissimilar to the space/object hybrid described by academics Colin Rowe and Fred Koetter in their book *Collage City*, largely acknowledges how space is a commodity worth preserving for its socio-environmental benefits (Rowe and Koetter, 1978). The inconvenient truth of global warming further reinforces the major role the new hybrid plays in the urban habitat and arguably defines a sixth generation in tall building design – that of a vertical reinterpretation of the compact city that embraces open space and its greenery as part of a vertical urban theory. It conceives the tall building from the inside out as opposed to the outside in. It is a process in which we also see space take precedence over form. After all, it is the provision of space that, in the first instance, can promote good health, enhance productivity and foster 'social well-being' of the individual, group or association. Space, in the second instance, can provide natural light, ventilation and opportunities for the replenishment of urban greenery for the benefit of the 'carbon well-being' of the built environment.

1.5 The birth of alternative social spaces

The slow eradication of public spaces that were once, amongst other things, venues for social interaction, trading and public debate saw its spatial replenishment come in the form of a variety of alternative spaces within historical and new building typologies – all of which were created to redress the changes in the public and private realms of society and its correlating need for space to socialise or retreat. The Habermasian public sphere of debate and discourse amongst civil society found outlet in the coffee houses and salons of 18th century Europe, which were further popularised by literacy improvements, accessibility to literature and a new critical journalism (Habermas, 1989). The privatisation of public spaces led buildings, such as the 18th century hotel, the 19th century arcade and the 20th century skyscraper, to start including social spaces that were not strictly public, yet bestowed elements of public life within them. The public realm of the street and square were soon accompanied by courts for meeting, arcades for circulation and promenading, internal streets and rooftop gardens for recreation to meet the increasing complexity of society's social needs. These managed 'social spaces' within the private ownership of landowners permitted accessibility to civil society, imbuing on the individual particular freedoms of expression but in the same instance an increased ambiguity as to what was and what was not permissible social behaviour. As the spaces remained outside the jurisdiction of the state, maintenance and policing had to be made by the owner, and effectively marked the arrival of a new spatial classification – that of the semi-public realm.

King François I's decision to make Paris the seat of government assured the development of a building typology that incorporated an element of social space. This came in the form of the 18th century hotel – an aristocratic residence, often located within the vicinity of the royal palace. The hotel contained a void space in the form of a court – a semi-public space where members of civil society could promenade, meet and greet within the private realm of the residence. Minor members of the aristocracy were therefore able to contribute to civil society through the philanthropic provision of social space that was policed, managed and maintained by their very owners (Dennis, 1986). The Baroque *Hotel de Beauvais*, Paris, by Antoine Le Pautre is a fine example (Figure 17). The figurative and symmetrical nature of

Figure 17: *Hotel de Beauvais*, Paris: the court formed an alternative social space that provided a destination space within the city

the court contrasted the irregularity of the encapsulating rooms that acted as the urban infill and took up the site's geometric idiosyncrasies, which were largely driven by the existing foundations of three medieval houses. The design represents a social change in the need for places of interaction, but in the same instance demonstrates the gradual spatial transformation of the urban environment from the predominance of the public figurative void space to the private iconic object in undifferentiated space. It is therefore analogous to the evolution from the traditional to the modern city.

The 19th century saw the creation of another building type that sought to address civil society's need for a managed alternative social space that permitted civil society to be actor and spectator in public – be they viewing manufactured goods, or being viewed by others promenading in the vicinity. The arcade incorporated a pedestrian thoroughfare between existing public squares or streets, and was bordered or covered by a building, which often had its own use. The type owed its success to being an 'object of speculation' that 'offer[ed] public space on private property as well as an easing of traffic congestion, a short cut, protection from the weather and an area accessible only to pedestrians. These advantages suggest[ed] financial success for the renters of the sites and finally for their owners' (Geist, 1983). The arcade developed to become an integral part of the urban fabric within the city and represented 'the larger interests of public life … endowing the pedestrian once again with his full import and becoming the driving force behind the reorganization of public space' (Geist, 1983). It is perhaps unsurprising that the arcade would become a symbol of cultural and economic progress for newly established nations – an unmistakable index of urban life and the prosperity of a city, as one can see in the Galleria Vittorio Emmanuelle II, Milan (Figure 18).

Figure 18: *Galleria Vittorio Emanuelle II*, Milan: a pedestrianised thoroughfare that provided a means of transition through the city

Much like the 19th century arcade, the 20th century skyscraper has similarly been an index of progress. Modern city planning saw the erosion of public space in favour of the private, object-driven building. High-rise structures sought to reconcile spatial loss by incorporating an element of social space within the private realm of the development, and in particular assigned it internally as streets or externally to the

Figure 19: *Unité d'habitation*, Marseilles: the 'social condenser' celebrated the rooftop as a means of recreation

rooftop (Figure 19). Le Corbusier's fifth point in *Vers une architecture* dictated the importance of rooftop terraces to not just replenish the area consumed by the building but also to provide space for social health and well-being (Frampton, 1992) – an ideal that was realised in *Unité d'habitation*. 'Uniting its 337 dwellings with a shopping arcade, a hotel and a roof deck, a running track, a paddling pool, a kindergarten and a gymnasium, the Unité was just as much of a "social condenser" as the soviet commune blocks of the 1920s. This total integration of community services recalled the 19th century model of Fourier's phalanstery, not only through its size but also in its isolation from the immediate environment' (Frampton, 1992).

The advent of the 18th century court, the 19th century arcade and the 20th century rooftop garden has progressively been joined by other social space models. The modern shopping mall goes beyond retail to embrace a multiplicity of function that can include healthcare, workplace, entertainment, leisure and convention uses that starts to position the object as a focal point of a community. The suburban mall can be viewed as a private alternative to the public market place and demonstrates how a managed social space can be incorporated into a private development in order to increase footfall and revenue generation (Figure 20). Private corporations contribute social spaces with public domain characteristics but go through a process of commodification in their ability to be rented out as venues for commercial enterprise. Such an approach has become a model for inner city retail development (Kohn, 2004).

As a response to privatisation, there has also been the need to view spaces as 'public goods' within privatised environments – often defended by economists as goods that may be of benefit to more than just the purchaser/consumer. The hotel lobby and the shopping mall atrium are key examples of privatised spaces that form a betterment levy – the price paid to the community in exchange for the increase in land value arising from its efforts when granted planning permission (Figure 21). The academic Brian Field argues that their provision can be justified in the same way that public space is defended as an essential requirement for the health and well-being of civil society (Field, 1992). Hotel lobbies have become the forum for business meetings

Figure 20: *Star Vista Mall*, Singapore: a private alternative to the public market place and town square

Figure 21: *Marina Bay Sands Hotel*, Singapore: an alternative social space that increasingly forms part of a betterment levy

and environments from which business transactions and wireless working can be conducted without the need for entering the confines of the office. Like the shopping mall, they permit entry to an individual who neither owns nor is resident, and yet is granted particular social freedoms of speech and action provided he or she conforms to the rules and regulations specified by the private entity that controls the space.

We have seen in this part how the public realm has been gradually eroded by Man, and how its privatisation has resulted in alternative social spaces that have offered spatial replenishment, but also explicit (and often limiting) rules of social engagement. The inclusion of such privately managed social spaces has reinforced a hierarchy of space within the urban habitat for the social interactions of its users. They seek to balance space within the object and recapture elements of public life within the private curtilage. In doing so, they form an accompaniment rather than a replacement to the traditional public domain of the street and square. Whilst public space has become synonymous with impersonal contact and relies on the individual's mask of civility to be able to interact in public, the semi-public domain of these alternative social spaces provides an opportunity to increase social networks. However, they have the potential to limit social freedoms (such as motion, speech and action), given their privatised and commoditised nature. With a continued pressure on both the private and public sectors to consider a socio-spatial sustainability in the interests of providing a 'public good' for society, skycourts and skygardens within tall buildings are increasingly becoming such an addition to the 21st century urban habitat's open space infrastructure, and continue the line of spatial development from their predecessors. We shall investigate this further in Part 2.

Defining the skycourt and skygarden

2. Defining the skycourt and skygarden

2.1 The skycourt and skygarden: a historical overview

There have been notable historical precedents that suggest skycourts and skygardens are not phenomenon only known in our lifetime, but can be found in the urban habitats of antiquity and the immediate past. We can trace the skygarden back to ancient civilisation's quest to integrate greenery into cities at height. The *Hanging Gardens of Babylon*, built by Nebuchadnezzar II for his wife Amyitis, were documented by the Greek historian Diodorus Siculus in the 6th century BC as being a series of planted terraces that were supported on stone arches 23 metres above ground. The Syrian King reputedly built the hanging gardens in an effort to please his homesick wife, who longed for her homeland of Persia. Trees were embedded into tiered stones terraces, with permanently green foliage made possible by a mechanical irrigation system from the Euphrates River.

Al-Fustat, an Egyptian city known for its shaded streets, gardens and markets that today forms part of Old Cairo, similarly incorporated skygardens. Modern archaeologists have recovered relics that came from as far as Spain, China, and Vietnam, providing evidence of the city's importance as a trade hub as well as being a production centre of Islamic art and ceramics. It was reputedly one of the wealthiest cities in the world and had an estimated population of 200,000 people (Mason, 1995). The Persian poet and philosopher Nasir Khusraw described the city as having a number of 14- storey high-rise residential buildings that were surmounted by recreational rooftop gardens that were customised by its inhabitants and irrigated by ox-drawn water wheels (Barghusen and Moulder, 2001; Behrens-Abouseif, 1992).

In Italy, hill towns such as Urbino and San Gimignano manipulated the natural topographic levels of their location to create urban settlements that were protected given their elevated position (Figure 22). During the Renaissance, steeply terraced gardens and green roofs were common in the city of Genoa. Raised piazzas, interconnected by steps to traverse the changes in level, permitted surveillance of the land beneath but also the environments for public events to take place (Peck *et al.*, 1999). At the private scale, the *Villa Giulia*, built between 1550 and 1555 by the architects Ammanati and Vignola for Pope Julius III, manipulated the natural topographic and man-made levels in order to allow the Pope and his entourage to enjoy views of the surrounding

Figure 22: *San Gimignano*, Siena: a lush and steeply terraced hill town in Italy with public spaces at multiple levels

landscape from its raised terraces and three-tiered covered loggias (Watkin, 2005).

Figure 23: *The Eiffel Tower*, Paris: a structure that permits the democratisation of view for the fee-paying visitor

By the 19th century, the ability to glean panoramic views was no longer the realm of the privileged few. The democratisation of view from ever-increasing heights, made possible by the invention of the elevator, further challenged any exclusive preconceptions of elevated levels by providing opportunities for society to survey the city as a means of recreation and delight. The *Eiffel Tower* of the Paris exposition of 1889 stood as a testimony to human ingenuity and technological advancement in an industrial age (Figure 23). It provided a platform from which people could marvel at the Paris skyline for an entrance fee, and remains the most visited paid monument in the world. Its ability to provide a panorama as a sellable commodity and thus a means of income generation has since become a template for many an observation gallery in tall buildings within cities around the world.

Figure 24: *Unité d'habitation*, Marseilles: recreational space on the roof to supplement open space on the ground

By the 20th century, the influence of Le Corbusier and his manifesto of celebrating the rooftop as a further means of supplementing those open recreational spaces on the ground further spawned examples of planted and unplanted sky-rise social spaces within an increasingly object-driven modern city (Figure 24). Architects such as Ken Yeang went further to adopt the skycourt as an interstitial open space within buildings for its environmental as well as socio-economic benefits, and the skycourt has become an increasingly important part of a new architectural vocabulary within high-density urban environments (Pomeroy, 2012a) (Figure 25). Norman Foster's *Commerzbank* in Frankfurt aptly demonstrates their incorporation. The tall building was conceived as three 'petals' of triangular office floor plates, grouped around a central 'stem' formed by a full-height atrium (Figure 26). Sealed skycourts of four storeys high rise up through the height of the building, rotating every four storeys to the next face. The skycourts provide employees with an opportunity to view other skycourts above and below, as well as the cityscape beneath and the sky above. These spaces provide a social dimension for the office employees to use as places of meeting, events, lunches or remote working. They have been described as a social foci 'with coffee bars and seating tucked amongst the plants. They are thus intrinsic to Foster's vision of the tower as a community of villages with each garden as a village square/green for the 240 employees who directly overlook it' (Davey, 1997).

Skycourts and skygardens continue to be part of the urban habitat today, and exist for the very same reasons that they did in antiquity. They are places of recreation for the individual or group, can afford a memorable view and vantage point, and can offer environmental as well as socio-physiological benefit. Yet despite such historical precedents and the important role that they play, little has been done to define skycourts and skygardens in terms of their spatial, social, economic, environmental, technological or cultural contribution, or the increasingly diverse role that they play within the urban habitat. The following sections will seek to define their multi-faceted nature.

Figure 25: *Menara Mesiniaga*, Kuala Lumpur: an early example of a tall building that incorporates skycourts for their social-environmental benefits

Figure 26: *Commerzbank*, Frankfurt: an exemplary environmentally responsive building that incorporates skycourts to form a vertical working village

2.2 The skycourt and skygarden: spatial morphology and perceived density

In urban terms, 'density' often carries the negative spatial and social connotation of the close proximity of buildings in one constrained location, or of cramped living conditions where there is a heightened proximity between individuals. According to the academic Vicky Cheng, perceived density refers to 'the interaction between the individual and the space, and between individuals in the space', which requires the concepts of spatial density ('the perception of density with respect to the relationship among spatial elements') and social density ('the interaction between people') to distinguish between the two different aspects of the former (Cheng, 2010). She points out that these definitions demonstrate how perceived densities straddle different disciplines under different contexts, and how urban density is intrinsically associated with the shaping and densification of urban morphology.

Society's aversion to urban density given pre-conceived notions that such environments lack space for interaction, or are homogenous environments that lack character, therefore requires careful consideration. This is because there are a myriad of high-density case studies that embody such attributes but are celebrated urban settings for their inhabitants and visitors alike (OECD, 2012). Hong Kong and Paris demonstrate this, and also how high-density urban habitats need not relate to just high-rise structures. An investigation into the spatial morphology of Hong Kong and Paris demonstrates that the iconic high-rise developments of the former may be perceived to be higher density than the lower-rise developments of the latter, and yet the reality is that Haussmann's 6–7 storey districts are in fact denser than a Hong Kong neighbourhood of 20 storeys (Figure 27). When comparing the two cities in terms of floor area ratio (FAR), Paris has an FAR of 5.75, whilst Hong Kong's is 4.32, demonstrating that higher densities can be achieved by alternative building forms to the high-rise typology, which can similarly reduce perceived densities (OECD, 2012) (Figure 28).

It perhaps comes as little surprise that the skycourt has become an increasingly important element within the architectural vocabulary of the world's tallest buildings and the densest environments as a means of reducing perceived densities. Skycourts can be initially defined in terms of their

Figure 27: Haussmann's Paris: a high-density environment of 6–7 storeys with an FAR of 5.75

Figure 28: A Hong Kong neighbourhood: a high-density environment of 20 storeys with an FAR of 4.32

spatial morphology and how they can reduce the perceived densities of a tall building, or high-density development, by breaking the mass and potential monotony of repetitive floor plates by the juxtaposition of solid and void (Pomeroy, 2005; 2007). They have the ability to evoke the human scale and proportion of the traditional street by presenting themselves within high-density urban habitats and tall buildings as interstitial open or enclosed spaces that balance the figurative (semi-public) void within the solid of the (private) object.

As the word 'court' suggests, a sense of enclosure can be created by the void space being bordered by other buildings within the immediate urban context, or formed by its own internal façades. Skycourts are often located at the perimeter of buildings and are commonly three storeys or more to allow the benefit of greater light and ventilation to penetrate deeper into the structure – thus enhancing the internal environment (Figure 29). Such proportions also permit, depending on orientation and climatic factors, the incorporation of trees or extensive landscaping to further enhance the aesthetic, socio-physiological and environmental properties of these social spaces.

Figure 29: *Mirador*, Sanchinarro: a mid-level hollowed out skycourt as an interstitial space

The rooftop garden has been defined as a landscaped environment built on the roof of a building that is strong enough to support the load, and is ideally suited to reinforced concrete and steel structures (Osmundson, 1999) (Figure 30). A skygarden, on the other hand, tends to refer to an open or enclosed landscaped open space that can be dispersed through the higher levels of the urban habitat or tall building, and has become a generic term that occasionally substitutes the terms skycourt and rooftop garden. As the name suggests, emphasis is often placed on the aesthetic qualities of the garden setting and its appeal to occupants. Just as one normally finds a proportion of open space to built-up area in ground-scraping mixed-use developments, skycourts and skygardens start to vertically balance open space to built-up area ratios within the tall building (Pomeroy, 2009).

Architects such as Stephen Holl have explored the de-densification of urban centres by the incorporation of skycourts, skygardens and skybridges, and in doing so have created hybrid structures that balance solid and void.

Figure 30: *Marina Barrage*, Singapore: an example of a rooftop skygarden that serves as a public park

The ability to explore vertical, diagonal and horizontal open space networks to reduce perceived densities substantially supports a mixed-use programme of activities that redefine the 24-hour city, and acts as a catalyst for spontaneity and interaction. Holl's *Linked Hybrid*, in Beijing, explores such a concept and acknowledges Beijing's change of urban morphology (Figure 31). What was historically a dense network of streets and courtyards was transformed post 1980s into a city of monotonous high-rise objects that expressed a greater verticality in the skyline (Per *et al.*, 2011). The Linked Hybrid conceptually seeks to reconcile the city of objects with a city of spaces by interlinking eight towers via a 20th-storey ring of skybridges that accommodate recreational and community-related facilities for both its occupants and visitors alike. The typically repetitive nature of the high-density residential development in the region is discarded in favour of a diversity of apartment configurations and sizes that are further spatially deconstructed by the presence of the skycourts that help reduce the perceived densities.

Figure 31 (top–bottom): *The Linked Hybrid*, Beijing: skycourts, skygardens and skybridges seek to reduce perceived densities

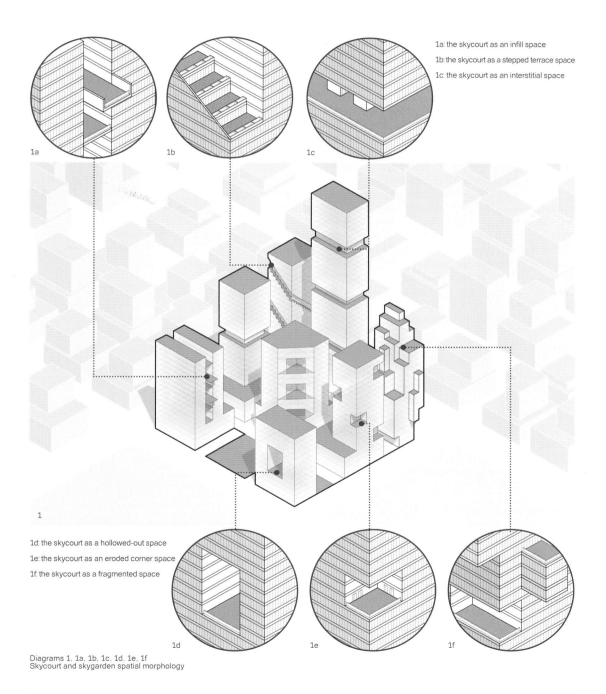

1a: the skycourt as an infill space

1b: the skycourt as a stepped terrace space

1c: the skycourt as an interstitial space

1a

1b

1c

1

1d: the skycourt as a hollowed-out space

1e: the skycourt as an eroded corner space

1f: the skycourt as a fragmented space

1d

1e

1f

Diagrams 1, 1a, 1b, 1c, 1d, 1e, 1f
Skycourt and skygarden spatial morphology

2.3 The skycourt and skygarden as a social space

The philosopher Henri Lefebrve stated that society produces its own spatial code that isolates and separates fragments of everyday life through boundaries, producing spaces specific to itself. The academic Ulrich Struver's notion of *critical spatial identities*, however, acknowledges relationships between groups as opposed to boundaries (Best and Struver, 2002). Groups may have different spatial interpretations of a given space which sets up power struggles, requiring one power to be dominant (appropriating the space in such a way that would be perceived as conventional); the others subservient (often perceived as unconventional). For instance, what may be used as a transitional space between buildings (as governed by an institution and perceived as the conventional) may also be used as a skateboarding area appropriated by a subculture (as appropriated by society and perceived as the unconventional) (Figure 32). Such an interdependence of dominant and subservient powers creates a formative tension that can be used as an instrument of power; the enforcing of such, whether by a private corporate body, council, individual, group or association being the device to control, maintain or manage.

Figure 32: *The South Bank Arts Complex*, London: a public space being appropriated as a skateboarding environment

Skycourts and skygardens can act as social spaces in the sky that help replenish the loss of open space potentially surrendered through urban densification. Like the street and the square, they are spaces that provide a forum for social interaction and can facilitate chance or planned meetings with others as well as a means of recreation. Like its public space counterpart, these skyrise spaces can permit communal groups to form and disband, and in so doing potentially present the contestation of its space over its function amongst social groups that meet regularly. For instance, students may gather within such spaces outside of school hours to share notes before disbanding; office workers may meet with fellow workers from different departments for coffee or lunch breaks, before returning to their respective departments within a working day; residents may populate these spaces during the weekend and/or in evenings to meet with neighbours and friends before retiring to their home, and tourist groups may gather to observe a panoramic view but will similarly disband upon closing time (Figure 33). Its continual use by a dominant individual, group or association can imprint an element of informal territoriality on a place that may implicitly restrict the use of the space by others.

Figure 33: *Ssamziegil*, Seoul: the skygarden as an informal gathering place for friends and shoppers

Figure 34: *The Pinnacle*, Singapore: explicit rules of governance that negate particular freedoms of speech, motion and action

Unlike their open space counterparts on the ground, which tend to be governed by public interests and permit a spontaneity and freedom of movement, speech and action, skycourts and skygardens are often semi-public and are governed by private interests. This in turn imparts particular social restrictions that are more formal. Despite bearing public domain characteristics that allow the user a particular freedom of movement or the ability to appropriate the space as a place of recreation, amenity and social interaction, they are nevertheless managed spaces that are physically constrained by the very structure that retains them and are controlled by the institution, company, association or group that governs the tall building (Pomeroy, 2012a). This inevitably leads to limitations on the patterns of speech and action of the individual, group and association appropriating the space given the dominant (private) party's control of the space (Figure 34). The resultant social spaces are often highly classified environments that have explicit rules of exclusion that may be time-based (i.e the operating hours of the corporation or the levying of an entrance fee) or implicit rules of inclusion that are based on social activity (i.e. to be part of a studying community; an office community; a residential community or a tourist community).

The Pinnacle, in Singapore, demonstrates such an approach in its ability to use 12 skygardens to interconnect its seven, 50-storey high-density social housing blocks comprising of 1,848 family units (Figure 35). The skygardens reinterpret the ground-level void decks of the past social housing blocks as a series of elevated social spaces. The intermediary gardens at the 26th floor serve the residents only, whilst the 50th-floor rooftop garden is accessible to the public in addition to residents. The 26th-storey intermediary gardens have explicit rules of governance as to who can enter and who cannot – they are ultimately privatised spaces for the sole use of its residents and are thus encoded with explicit rules of exclusion, despite being deemed public by the state. Its 50th-storey skygarden, again deemed public, also has explicit rules of governance but is encoded with implicit rules of exclusion with the proposed levying of an entrance fee to gain access to it as an observation deck. Those who can afford to pay for a view will enjoy a panoramic skyline; those who will not or cannot will be excluded by their own choice or economic circumstance. Thus, in this case, it could be argued that the freedom of passage and ability to appropriate the rooftop space as one feels free to socialise in the public domain of the street and square runs the risk of being nullified; not, as one would assume, by private interests anxious at the preservation of their asset, but paradoxically by state governance that would under normal circumstances promote greater levels of inclusivity in the use of open space by local and visitor, resident and non-resident (Pomeroy, 2011).

Figure 35 (top–bottom): *The Pinnacle*, Singapore: an example of how skycourts can act as the new social spaces for residents to enjoy

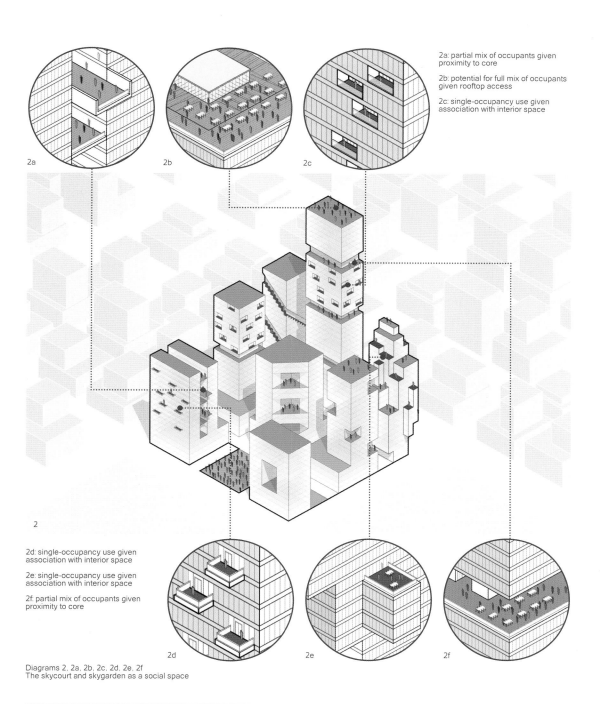

2a: partial mix of occupants given proximity to core

2b: potential for full mix of occupants given rooftop access

2c: single-occupancy use given association with interior space

2a

2b

2c

2

2d: single-occupancy use given association with interior space

2e: single-occupancy use given association with interior space

2f: partial mix of occupants given proximity to core

2d

2e

2f

Diagrams 2, 2a, 2b, 2c, 2d, 2e, 2f
The skycourt and skygarden as a social space

2.4 The skycourt as a transitional space

According to the academic Arnis Siksna, when inner cities become denser and pedestrian movement increases, the two-dimensional plane of the city reaches its elastic limit. It forces the city to move to a second stage of development, whereby it can take no more growth without incorporating auxiliary systems and layers, such as transit, parking and subways, to facilitate choice and freedom of movement (Siksna, 1998). This inevitably thrusts itself into the third dimension in order to cater for increased density and movement. A city like Hong Kong, with its myriad of skyways, bridge links and multi-layered movement systems above and below ground, cannot reach such a threshold of movement needed to expand into the third dimension unless it has the pre-requisite urban density of its centre to sustain an increase in population (Figure 36). Without such infrastructure, the compact city would run the risk of accessibility suffocation due to its own success (Gabay and Aravot, 2003).

Figure 36: Central mid-level escalators, Hong Kong: a city that has embraced multi-level movement systems to address accessibility suffocation

Similarly, the tall building typology cannot reach the threshold needed to expand skywards into the third dimension unless it has the pre-requisite skycourts and auxiliary systems (i.e. the deployment of underground trains, parking structures, skybridges and other technical facilities) to sustain an increase in occupancy or pedestrian flow. Without such infrastructure, the compact city of objects would similarly run the risk of accessibility suffocation. The need for improved circulatory methods to facilitate an ease of pedestrian movement at height, is as pertinent in the tall building typology as it is to the urban environment at grade, and reinforces the importance of ensuring an equality of movement for civil society in the sky as well as on the ground.

The skycourt can act as a transitional space in its ability to be a circulatory interchange in super-tall buildings, whereby lift car capacities, waiting times and floor plate efficiencies necessitate the stacking of local lift cores to enhance the economic viability of the development. Just as civil society is provided with both choice of route and mode of transport on the ground (the ability to walk, cycle, drive, or take public transport through a variety of axes), the occupant or visitor is faced with a multiplicity of circulation routes and modes in the sky, making the skycourt not only a destination place of recreation and planned meeting, but also a transitional space of movement and chance meeting (Pomeroy, 2008)

Figure 37: *Taipei 101*, Taipei: transfer floors are expanded to be hubs of interaction between different functions

Figure 38: *Selfridges*, Birmingham: transitional spaces and bridge links that function as pseudo-vertical arcades

(Figure 37). Consequently, the incorporation of skycourts can facilitate the occupants' onward transition from one part of the tall building to another, by linking the disparate vertical circulation modes, and even to other buildings and their skycourts (Wood, 2003). The skycourt acts as a pseudo-vertical arcade by its ability to link primary, secondary and tertiary modes of vertical circulation.

The incorporation of retail compounds the analogy further – the skycourt being the (vertical) arcade; the lifts, escalators, staircases, ramps and other (vertical) circulation means being the hierarchical orders of boulevards, streets and passageways. It begins to ameliorate the risks of visual disconnection and separation from the activity of the street at ground level, as the horizontal and vertical means of circulation within a complex of tall buildings serves to create new eyes on the street in the sky, which can serve to aid security through the recognition of who is a stranger and who is not. It further harnesses the sense of community fostered through the movement of pedestrians, workers and residents from different parts of the tall building and beyond. Furthermore, it presents an opportunity to escape from one tall building into another via skybridge (Figure 38). Since the September 11 terrorist attacks, there has been a radical re-evaluation of mass evacuation procedures from tall buildings – thus ameliorating the need for phased evacuation which can compromise life safety and be economically unviable due to the increase in escape stairs required and therefore net-to-gross floor efficiencies (Wood, 2003).

The Shard London Bridge demonstrates how skycourts can be incorporated at mid-level as a transitional space (Figure 39). The 72-storey tower is the tallest mixed-use structure in Europe and stands at over 310 metres tall. The first 26 floors above the public piazza houses 55,551 square metres of modern high-specification office space with winter gardens. A five-star hotel with 202 rooms from the 34th to the 52nd floors, and residential apartments from the 53rd to the 65th, complete the programme. Separating the working from the living spaces is a three-storey skycourt that acts not only as the community space that gels the disparate functions together, but also as a means of transition between them. It forms an effective interchange point amongst different social functions that starts to imprint a 24-hour city quality. Such a space is designed to provide memorable views of London for its 800,000 visitors per year, and contains retail, bars, restaurants, leisure, performance and exhibition activities as well as social spaces for the tower's inhabitants and the broader community. It effectively becomes a new square in the sky – a place of orientation, chance or planned meeting and onward journey to one's destination via the multiple vertical transportation routes within the building's core.

Figure 39: (top–bottom) *The Shard*, London: its mid-level skycourt acts as a transitional space as well as a destination space

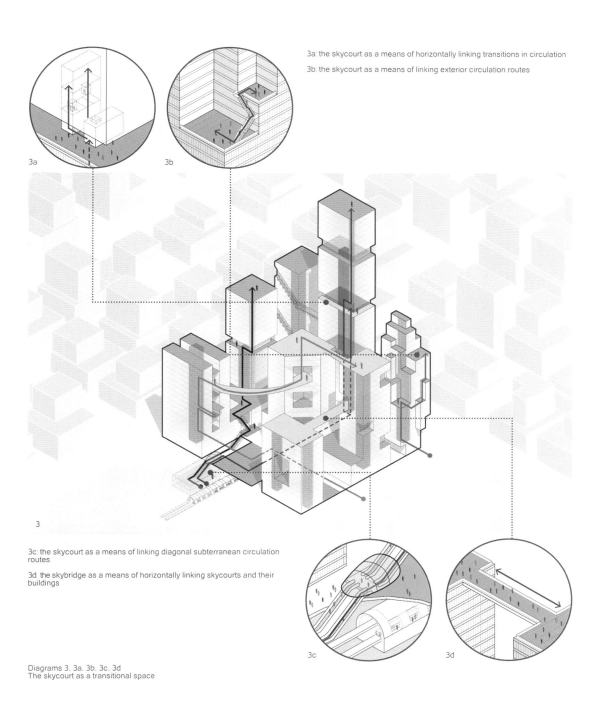

3a: the skycourt as a means of horizontally linking transitions in circulation

3b: the skycourt as a means of linking exterior circulation routes

3a

3b

3

3c: the skycourt as a means of linking diagonal subterranean circulation routes

3d: the skybridge as a means of horizontally linking skycourts and their buildings

3c

3d

Diagrams 3, 3a, 3b, 3c, 3d
The skycourt as a transitional space

2.5 The skycourt and skygarden as an environmental filter

Natural light and ventilation are essential for the survival of living organisms. Builders of traditional buildings understood the importance of harvesting natural light and ventilation before Man's technological ingenuity led to inventions that removed the need to rely on a proximity to perimeter windows. As noted by the academic Rayner Banham in *The Architecture of the Well-Tempered Environment*, by the turn of the 19th century the architect had ceded such environmental considerations to the consulting engineer (Banham, 1984). Today, however, both academics and professionals alike have returned to the basics of passive design, in order to enhance internal comfort levels and reduce consumption in buildings. We see such considerations of filtering the benefits of natural light and ventilation through open spaces such as arcades and atria, though arguably this requires heightened glass performance and/or shading devices to counteract the potential heat gain through direct solar exposure (Figure 40).

Figure 40: *Allen Lambert Galleria*, Toronto: a structure that provides natural light but necessitates shading to counteract direct solar heat gain

Incorporating skycourts as interstitial openings at the perimeter of buildings provides an alternative aperture to atria that permits natural light and ventilation to penetrate deeper into the floor plate whilst avoiding overhead direct solar heat gain. Daylight design best practice guidelines suggest that natural light can penetrate a space from a single side by up to 2.5 times the floor-to-ceiling height (Baker and Steemers, 2000). Therefore, a skycourt with a floor-to-ceiling height of 6 metres should be able to permit up to 15 metres of daylight penetration, thus helping reduce the reliance on artificial lighting means. The appropriate orientation of skycourts is, however, required in order to provide an 'environmental filter' that can mitigate low-angle sun and the potential for noise and high-speed wind penetration. This is because the greater wall surface area exposed to climatic factors, as a result of incorporating skycourts, may also be to the detriment of a building's environmental performance (Puteri and Ip, 2006).

The incorporation of greenery to skycourts and skygardens can counteract such issues given the ability of plants to reduce external climatic factors. Greenery to the horizontal and vertical surfaces of skycourts and skygardens can help reduce urban heat island effect, the absorption of heat in the building fabric, and its subsequent re-radiation by harnessing the biological properties of plants – such as photosynthesis, respiration, transpiration and evaporation (Figure 41). Planted

Figure 41: *Acros Building*, Fukuoka: greening vertical and horizontal surfaces can help reduce ambient temperatures

surfaces can help cool the environment by 3.6–11.3 degrees centigrade, with wall surfaces being reduced by as much as 12 degrees centigrade (Alexandri and Jones, 2008; Wong *et al.*, 2009). When trees are positioned at the perimeter of skycourts, they can act as a shading device, with light tree canopies intercepting between 60% and 80% of sunlight and dense canopies intercepting as much as 98% (Johnston and Newton, 2004). They can also help act as a wind-break and thus reduce loading to structural frames. They also form an effective acoustic buffer to urban noise. Vertical planting, the trapped layer of air between the plants and the substrate can help absorb, reflect and deflect sound waves, and reduce low-frequency noise by as much as 9.9 dB (Wong *et al.*, 2010) (Figure 42).

Planted skycourts and skygardens can also improve air quality and help reduce respiratory illnesses by acting as a 'sponge' to noxious pollutants and carbon dioxide in the atmosphere, with climbing plants showing a particular susceptibility to absorbing and filtering dust particles. Urban settings with trees may reduce dust particles to 1,000–3,000 dust particles per litre, whilst an environment with no trees may contain 10,000–12,000 dust particles per litre (Johnston and Newton, 2004). They also have the added ecological benefit of retaining storm water, thus helping reduce run-off into drains and the occurrence of flash floods during extreme rain periods. Studies in Berlin showed that green roofs absorb 75% of precipitation that falls upon them, reducing immediate rainwater discharge by 25% of normal levels whilst helping remove impurities. The filtration properties of plants can remove over 95% of cadmium, copper and lead from rainwater and 16% of zinc, whilst nitrogen levels can also be reduced (Johnston and Newton, 2004).

Ken Yeang's *Singapore National Library* aptly demonstrates the incorporation of planted skycourts for such environmental benefits (Figure 43). The tall building consists of two blocks that are separated by a naturally lit internal street with connecting bridges, escalators and lifts to the upper levels. The library has over 6,300 square metres (or 11% of the total gross floor area) of designated green space that acts as an environmental filter to the low-angled east and west orientated sun. This helps reduce solar heat gain and provides an effective shading device. Of the 14 skycourts and

Figure 42: *Orchard Central*, Singapore: applying vertical greenery to reduce heat and noise generated by mechanical plant areas

skygardens, there are two main areas situated on the fifth and tenth floors. These contain 12-metre-high trees that increase bio-diversity, help retain water on site and can also help regulate the ecosystem by acting as a respiratory system and filter of noxious pollutants. The provision of the skycourts, their greenery and the building's bio-climatic design considerations help enhance the indoor thermal performance and its energy efficiency. When compared with a typical Singaporean commercial building's energy consumption of 230 kWh/sqm/annum, the library has been able to reduce its consumption by 78 kWh/sqm/annum to give an energy consumption of 152 kWh/sqm/annum – making it one of the most energy-efficient buildings in Singapore (NLB, 2008).

Figure 43 (top–bottom): *National Library*, Singapore: the skycourt as an exemplary environmental filter

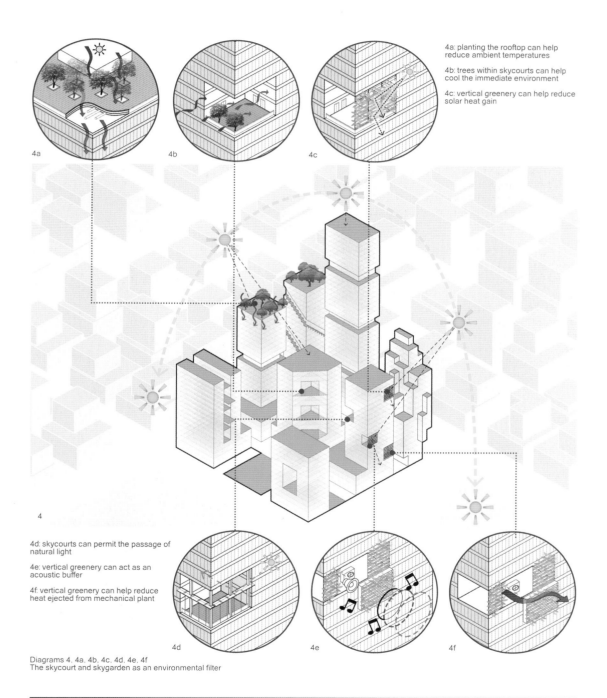

4a: planting the rooftop can help reduce ambient temperatures

4b: trees within skycourts can help cool the immediate environment

4c: vertical greenery can help reduce solar heat gain

4a

4b

4c

4

4d: skycourts can permit the passage of natural light

4e: vertical greenery can act as an acoustic buffer

4f: vertical greenery can help reduce heat ejected from mechanical plant

4d

4e

4f

Diagrams 4, 4a, 4b, 4c, 4d, 4e, 4f
The skycourt and skygarden as an environmental filter

2.6 The skycourt and skygarden: enhancing psycho-physiological well-being

An increased interest in the way that people process scenes formed the basis of a number of psychological studies held during the 1960s that considered what constituted beauty and what structural elements (for instance, boundary sharpness, complexity and light patterns) influenced people's perception of what is beautiful. Nature, or natural scenes, significantly influenced view preference scores, with people considering a scene as being natural 'if it contained predominantly vegetation and/or water, and if man-made features such as buildings or cars are absent or inconspicuous' (Ulrich, 1981, 1986). Such findings spurred further research into the psycho-physiological effects nature has on the individual, and considerations as to how it can help improve the mental state of health.

The academic Roger Ulrich's research further suggested that natural elements in the urban landscape counteracted physiological stress reactions through a stream of instantaneous affective (emotional) reactions (Ulrich, 1983). Studies of videotaped natural scenes were shown to speed physical and emotional recovery for traumatised people through nature's restorative power, by triggering quick, positive emotions to help reduce physiological stress. 'Findings were consistent with the predictions of the psycho-evolutionary theory that restorative influences of nature involve a shift towards a more positively-toned emotional state, positive changes in physiological activity levels, and that these changes are accompanied by sustained attention/intake' (Ulrich et al., 1990). Prisoners with windows facing surrounding hills were found to visit the infirmary with stress-related illnesses less frequently than those facing interior spaces, which further supports the hypotheses of the healing properties of nature (Moore, 1982).

The motivational qualities of viewing greenery have also been shown to positively affect task performance and mood (Shibata and Suzuki, 2002). Nature also has the ability to revive a person's concentration. Attention restoration theory suggests the mind's ability to avoid distraction can become exhausted with time. Direct attention, an inhibitory quality that can cause irritability, unwillingness to participate in group activity and inappropriate behaviour can be treated by focusing on natural environments that are rich in such qualities and can provide stimulation, but place no demands

Figure 44: *The Pinnacle@Duxton*, Singapore: an abundance of rooftop terraces provides inhabitants with social spaces in which to interact

on a person's ability to maintain concentration, in order to help ameliorate such reactions (Kaplan, 1995).

Landscaping has therefore been increasingly included in the design of skycourts and skygardens for not only their environmental benefits, but for their visual attributes that have been proven to enrich people's psycho-physiological well-being. Within a residential setting, landscaped skycourts and skygardens can encourage people to spend more time outdoors undertaking social and recreational activities, and thus heighten the likelihood of social interaction through chance meeting (Figure 44). This is particularly the case where trees have been found to act as a catalyst for congregation amongst a mix of ages and social groups, and can positively affect people's attitude to safety and adjustment in fostering a sense of community (Kuo *et al.*, 1998). This can result in heightened neighbourhood satisfaction and stronger social ties that can help protect the public welfare of the community. When incorporated into the workplace, skycourts and skygardens provide alternative informal working environments and places for meeting that can enhance productivity through the propagation of regular breaks outside of the formal office setting (Figure 45). They can also help foster inter-departmental social activity by acting as 'neutral' places to meet, that need not bear any particular departmental territoriality. In doing so, it can foster a greater sense of workplace community that can improve performance and productivity. The presence of greenery furthermore helps remove any noxious pollutants and heat released from computers, and offers visual relief from the workplace. In a healthcare setting, skycourts and skygardens similarly provide environments conducive to recuperation for the patient, but can also be places for healthcare staff to privately retreat, recuperate or socially interact in (Figure 46).

In the case of *Bedok Court*, a Singaporean residential development that dedicates 30–40% of its built-up area to skycourts, the academic Joo Hwa Bay found that 86% of the inhabitants used the skycourts for social purposes. A similarly high percentage found that they came into visual or physical contact with their neighbours through such spaces. The stepping of the skycourts also allowed 66% of the residents to interact with other neighbours on different levels.

Figure 45: *Genzyme*, Boston: a research environment in which skycourts act as breakout social spaces

Figure 46: *Venice-Mestre Hospital*, Venice: a healthcare environment that uses greenery to improve psychological well-being of the individual

This was attributed to the increased visual field through the staggered arrangement that allowed visual permeability (Figure 47). Bay's social survey was supplemented by a climatic survey, whereby residents' votes for thermal comfort were plotted against radiant temperature for morning, afternoon and evening. With the average radiant temperature of the skycourts being 28.5 degrees centigrade, a humidity level of 61% and a wind speed of 0.75 m/s, 70%–80% of the community felt slightly warm, comfortable or slightly cool for the three periods. The skycourt proved cooler than the external environment and only slightly warmer than the internal. Similar quantitative tests were undertaken for daylight factor and acoustics, which were then compared to the qualitative responses of residents. Bay asserted that the good thermal, acoustic and daylight properties of the skycourts created conducive environments for social interaction even during the hottest month (June) of the year. He concluded that such socio-climatic properties allowed the skycourts to promote community life as well as enhanced physiological well-being (Bay, 2004).

Figure 47 (top–bottom): *Bedok Court*, Singapore: generous skycourts allow homeowners to customise their space

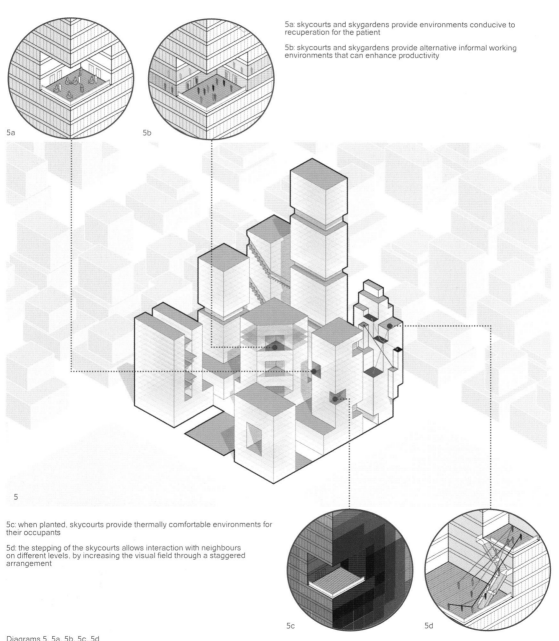

5a: skycourts and skygardens provide environments conducive to recuperation for the patient

5b: skycourts and skygardens provide alternative informal working environments that can enhance productivity

5a

5b

5

5c: when planted, skycourts provide thermally comfortable environments for their occupants

5d: the stepping of the skycourts allows interaction with neighbours on different levels, by increasing the visual field through a staggered arrangement

5c

5d

Diagrams 5, 5a, 5b, 5c, 5d
The skycourt and skygarden: enhancing psycho-physiological well-being

2.7 The skycourt and skygarden as a bio-diversity enhancer

The term 'bio-diversity' has a multitude of definitions relating to different scientific disciplines. Geneticists define it as the diversity of genes and organisms, whilst biologists define it as the accumulation of insects, fungi, plants, birds, animals and micro-organisms, their genetic and phenotypic variation and the manner in which they co-inhabit the Earth (Dirzo and Mendoza, 2008). In the urban habitat, bio-diversity refers to the quantification of habitable areas, and the diverse range of species and life forms that exist within (Currie and Bass, 2010). Such definitions demonstrate a commonality that bio-diversity is the degree of variation in life forms within a given ecosystem by which a measure of an ecosystem's health can be determined. The existence of such diverse life forms, each functioning and interconnecting with other organisms in life and death, creates a perpetual yet structured life-cycle that defines the level of bio-diversity within an ecosystem (Currie and Bass, 2010).

The consequent removal of greenery to make way for urban development has resulted in the reduction of bio-diversity to urban areas, and has necessitated the restoration, preservation and enhancement of bio-diversity to counteract the potential environmental ills caused by urban development. Bio-diversity within the urban habitat has often been manifested in the form of greenery through the planting of horizontal, diagonal and vertical surfaces. In doing so, the ability to increase a city's bio-diversity through the incorporation of skycourts and skygardens provides an opportunity to enhance the quality of life of urban dwellers as well as become an educational tool on urban sustainability-related issues (Hui and Chan, 2011).

One of the most common areas of exploitation is the rooftop – an environment often perceived as a non-accessible, undervalued part of the city. Green roofs, be they intensive (having depths of between 150 and 1,000 millimetres and a greater depth of growing medium to support a wider range of planting that includes shrubs and trees), extensive (having depths of between 50 to 150 millimetres and with low-growing plants, with no access other than for occasional maintenance) or brown (a non-seeded green roof system that undergoes natural colonisation with little human interaction, allowing local plant species to populate the roof over time) can help restore the imbalance of the

Figure 48: *PF-1 (Public Farm-1)*, New York: provides an alternative food source and promotes social interaction through collaborative farming

Figure 49: *Solaris Research Centre*, Singapore: bio-diverse eco-corridors reach up into the sky

Figure 50: The *Highline*, Manhattan: reinstating urban greenery to enhance the bio-diversity of this former railway track

urban ecosystem by providing habitats for the coexistence of insects, birds, plants, vertebrates and invertebrate animal species within the urban environment. They can also be an important agricultural source. With the continued trend of migration to city centres and consequent spatial shortage, the conversion of existing rooftops to create urban agriculture has made them an important alternative food source that centralises food production in growing compact cities. Such an approach helps reduce the reliance on rural agricultural means, its energy consumption and waste in food transportation (Figure 48).

When considered holistically as part of an urban green programme, skycourts and skygardens provide pockets of urban greenery that can create islands of bio-diversity within the city and replace the natural habitats lost through development. They can enhance the bio-diversity in urban centres by helping replenish the loss of urban greenery and at the same time provide a home for a greater breadth of wildlife. Skycourts and skygardens can provide a nesting ground for small birds and can in turn attract butterflies and insects through the right selection of plants that are rich in fruit and flowers (Chiang and Tan, 2009). Their soil can provide a home for spiders, beetles and ants, whilst the presence of nectar can attract insects such as bees and butterflies to as high as 20 storeys (Johnston and Newton, 2004). Vertical and diagonal greenery within skycourts can also provide linkage between the horizontal planes, and therefore form a natural continuum of the natural environment and a transitional route for wildlife (Figure 49). In doing so, skycourts and skygardens facilitate an approach to urban greenery that can be conceived as a continuous green vein within the city, and with it the opportunity for bio-diverse eco-corridors that transcend the ground plane by reaching up into the sky. This can help establish a larger network of wildlife eco-corridors in urban and suburban areas that help stitch and integrate larger, bio-diverse places, such as parks and gardens (Figure 50).

The 'Supertrees' of the *Gardens by the Bay* development in Singapore start to consider the sense of vertical green continuity in order to enhance the bio-diversity in city centres (Figure 51). Whilst not necessarily tall buildings, their extruded forms are nevertheless deliberate attempts to create green structures that would be in keeping with the scale, height and materiality of the surrounding tall building developments of the Marina Bay Financial District in Singapore. The public garden is punctuated by 18 of these man-made, tree-like structures of reinforced concrete, trunk, planting and canopy – 12 of which are contained in the Supertree grove, and a further six placed in clusters of three in the Golden and Silver Gardens. Ranging in heights of between 25 and 50 metres, they provide a home for an extensive array of localised species of wildlife, totalling over 162,900 plants and comprising 200 different species of bromeliads, orchids, ferns and tropical flowering climbers. Not only do the structures enhance the bio-diversity of the place, they also demonstrate an array of green technologies that seek to reduce waste, re-use water and recycle bio-matter for the preservation of other species inhabiting the structures as part of a broader eco-system life-cycle.

Figure 51 (top–bottom): Supertrees at *Gardens by the Bay*, Singapore: an urban opportunity to enhance bio-diversity

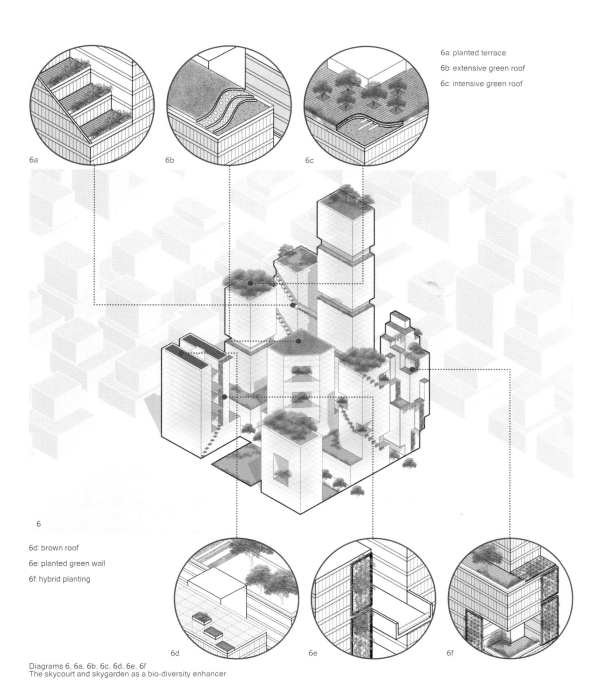

6a: planted terrace

6b: extensive green roof

6c: intensive green roof

6a

6b

6c

6

6d: brown roof

6e: planted green wall

6f: hybrid planting

6d

6e

6f

Diagrams 6, 6a, 6b, 6c, 6d, 6e, 6f
The skycourt and skygarden as a bio-diversity enhancer

2.8 The skycourt and skygarden: their economic benefits

In a time of increasing global environmental and social consciousness, the need to challenge the preconceived ideas of the 20th century tall building has led to a paradigm shift in tall building design that re-evaluates structure, envelope and the functional programme of uses. This has been in the interests of minimising consumption and preserving the natural and built environment for future generations. Such a shift has economic benefits. Skycourts and skygardens are increasingly important components within the architectural vocabulary of the sustainable tall building typology that can help reduce energy loads within buildings, whilst being an income-generating source that can attract people not normally associated with the development.

The environmental properties of greenery incorporated into skycourts and skygardens can reap benefits in terms of reduced energy consumption and therefore running costs. Rooftop gardens and their greenery have been shown to reduce ambient temperatures given plants' ability to absorb solar radiation (Figure 52). Studies have demonstrated that the exposed area of a black roof can reach 80 degrees centigrade, whilst an equivalent area beneath grass reaches only 27 degrees centigrade (Gotze, 1988; Kaiser, 1981). Gravel roofs have been shown to have temperatures of 30 degrees centigrade in comparison to 26 degrees centigrade for a green roof (Kaiser, 1981). The insulation properties of green roofs can reduce room temperatures beneath the structure by as much as 10%, thus helping to reduce artificial cooling and therefore running costs. When we also consider the shading properties of vertical planting within skycourts, Envelope Thermal Transfer Values (ETTV) can be reduced by 40% in comparison to a conventional building with no greenery (Chiang and Tan, 2009).

Figure 52: *Nanyang Technical University*, Singapore: the green roof as a means of reducing energy consumption

Yet skycourts and skygardens can also extend beyond their energy-reducing benefits to embrace direct income generation through their space provision. With continued urbanisation, the need to utilise available space becomes paramount. The ability to 'future-proof' developments by incorporating skycourts and skygardens provides opportunities to extend into the voids of skycourts, and into the airspace above skygardens in order to increase buildable area and therefore locally increase density (Figure 53). Such an approach optimises existing structures and can potentially

Figure 53: *Ontario College of Art and Design*, Toronto: exploiting the air rights above an existing building to increase density

Figure 54: *Red Sky*, Bangkok: A rooftop restaurant that manipulates views of the Bangkok skyline to be an income-generating destination

increase sellable and lettable areas of development whilst negating the need to demolish existing buildings and to rebuild – a process that can be potentially detrimental to the natural and built environment as well as to existing communities (Pomeroy, 2012b).

Their social function of providing a source of amenity can similarly offer economic benefits if incorporated midpoint within the building. They can be a useful source of convenience, recreation and amenity that can negate the need to travel groundwards for the grocery run, gymnasium visit or relaxation in open space. The critical mass of social and recreational activities, freed from the conventional setting of the ground plane, can enhance the footfall of the building's occupants at height, thus providing opportunities for passing trade and income generation (Pomeroy, 2012a). Just as research has shown how public space on the ground enhances property values, so too can skyrise social spaces command a premium.

Given rooftop skygardens' elevated position at the pinnacle of tall buildings, they can also function as observation decks, bars and restaurants that can be income-generating (Figure 54). The *Empire State Building* famously weathered the storm of financial crisis in the great depression through its 86th-floor observation deck that drew tourist receipts of $2 million in the first year of opening – as much money as was taken in rent that year (Tauranac, 1997). At the turn of the 21st century, there has been an unprecedented number of tall buildings of over 200 metres that have allowed Man to satiate his appetite for cityscape views in the form of observation decks. Rooftop skygardens therefore provide an opportunity to observe memorable skylines and panoramic views and the ability for people to pause and orientate themselves within both building and urban context. In doing so, they can potentially become a source of income by levying an entrance fee.

The *Marina Bay Sands*, Singapore, is a contemporary success story of the income-generating attributes of skycourts and skygardens (Figure 55). It is an integrated resort that accommodates up to 52,000 people. The three prominent hotel towers stand at 57 storeys and are crowned by a skypark, 191 metres above the ground. The 1.2 hectare park is the world's largest public cantilever and hosts a variety of amenities, including the longest elevated swimming pool of 146 metres amongst a lush tropical landscape setting. The skygarden is open daily from 9:30am to 10pm and can cater for up to 3,900 people at any one time. It has become an income generator through the levying of an entrance fee of 10–20 SGD per person to gain panoramic views of Singapore's skyline from its observation deck, generating an income of 54,600–78,000 SGD per day[4]. It also includes a number of rooftop bars, restaurants and shops that are positioned within the gardens. These have become a popular destination as it provides an alternative environment for locals and tourists alike to socially interact during the course of the day and through to the night, whilst its rooftop pool and performance areas provide further means of recreation and amenity for fee-paying guests.

Figure 55: *Marina Bay Sands*, Singapore: the 1.2 ha skypark is the world's largest public cantilever

(4) MBS interview 2012

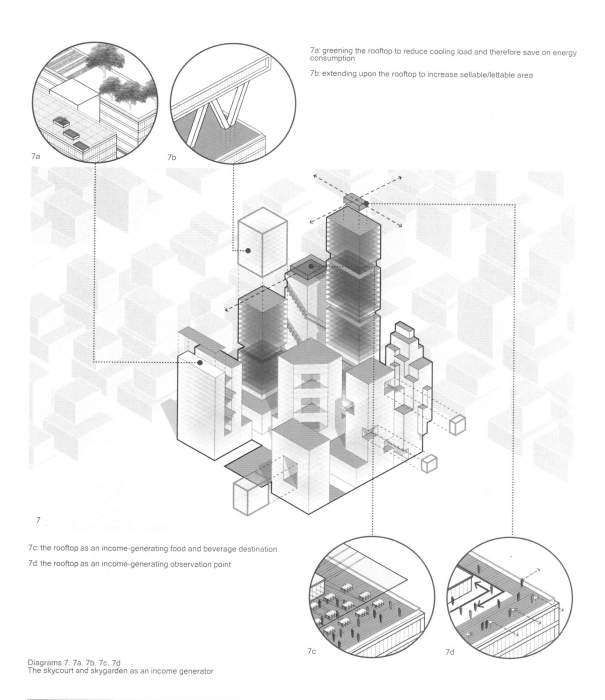

7a: greening the rooftop to reduce cooling load and therefore save on energy consumption

7b: extending upon the rooftop to increase sellable/lettable area

7

7c: the rooftop as an income-generating food and beverage destination

7d: the rooftop as an income-generating observation point

7a

7b

7c

7d

Diagrams 7, 7a, 7b, 7c, 7d
The skycourt and skygarden as an income generator

2.9 The skycourt and skygarden as part of a new legislated urban vocabulary

European and American planning policies that have encompassed urban renewal, construction, open space, nature conservation and drainage have all found relevance in shaping (almost literally) a greener urban habitat. We can see this in Germany, where legislated green roof construction, on all new-build development, has spawned an entire service industry. This has led to green-roof coverage increasing by approximately 13.5 million square metres per year (Haemmerle, 2002). In Chicago, and following the installation of its first rooftop garden on City Hall, more than 250 gardens and green roofs covering over 250,000 square metres have been constructed on schools, garages, museums and retail establishments (Daley and Johnson, 2008) (Figure 56). Despite the enviro-economic benefits that have seen green roofs celebrated, the ability to embrace the socio-economic agenda of creating alternative 'green' social spaces at height has been legislated significantly less, as can be seen in the scant guidance on the design and implementation of skycourts and skygardens.

Figure 56: *City Hall*, Chicago: Mayor Daley's vision of greening the city started with his administrative building

The UK's plethora of reports published by the Commission for Architecture and the Built Environment (CABE), such as the *Better Public Spaces* manifesto, have all aimed to create a national consensus that good-quality civic spaces should be a political and financial priority. The manifesto further advocates the importance of creating public spaces in order to improve the quality of life. We similarly see this in CABE's *Guide for Tall Buildings*, and in particular its reference to the importance of including public space as an integral part of tall building developments (CABE, 2007). Yet it does not go further than offering 'best practice' recommendations when designing tall buildings or, more crucially at a time of increasing urban densification, offering better alternative sky-rise social spaces to support the public spaces on the ground, as a means of socio-spatial replenishment. It re-affirms the absence of legislation in Europe and America regarding the incorporation of skycourts and skygardens as part of a broader open space framework within the urban habitat, despite their important role. In the case of Europe, this is perhaps understandable given the preservation of historical buildings that, according to the architectural critic Aaron Betsky, has led to the generic European city becoming an 'urban museum', filled with built artefacts that cater for nostalgia tourism and its associated income generation (Betsky, 2005).

It perhaps comes as little surprise that the spatial, social and environmental properties of skycourts and skygardens have instead influenced the planning legislation of more high-density urban environments, such as Singapore. Historically, the Singapore government's development charges were based on overall development area, which is the summation of both habitable and common areas. Developers would therefore seek to minimise common areas and maximise the habitable (sellable) areas in the interests of improving economic returns on their investment. In the interests of reducing perceived densities, promoting social interaction and well-being for occupants, and offering greater environmental benefits to the built environment, the Urban Redevelopment Authority (the government agency responsible for the urban planning of Singapore) passed urban policy that promoted the incorporation of skycourts and skygardens as permissible common area that would be exempt from the overall development area calculation.

The policy effectively sees the concept of a 45-degree line taken from the underside of any permanent or opaque structure as the means of highlighting the area exempt from the area calculation, and therefore from the development charges. The 45-degree line permits the penetration of light and the greater floor-to-ceiling height of the aperture (i.e a taller skycourt), the greater the permissible area exempt from development charges (Figure 57). This benefits the developer by the reduction of development charges whilst benefiting users in the incorporation of well-lit, recreational open space.

They are, however, subject to the following conditions: (1) the skycourt must be accessible to all occupants, (2) access to the skycourt must be from common areas only, (3) the skycourt is used for communal activities or for landscaping, (4) at least 40% of the perimeter wall of a skycourt must be open (Figure 58). Additional residual areas falling outside the 45-degree line can also be exempted, with a cap of 20% of the same floor plate, subject to the following criteria: (1) the areas within the 45-degree line must occupy at least 60% of the floor plate, and the remaining 40% (max) can be used for complementary uses, (2) the residual area must form an integral part of the skycourt remaining unenclosed, communal and non-commercial in nature, (3) at least 60%

Figure 57: *One George Street*, Singapore: CapitaCommercial Trust's office tower, located in the central business district, demonstrates the 45-degree rule to create a skygarden

Figure 58: *Newton Suites*, Singapore: an example of skycourts acting as communal space that would be exempt from overall development area calculation

of the perimeter of the skycourt should be kept open with low walls (URA, 2008) (Figure 59). The government's introduction of *Landscaping for Urban Spaces and High Rises* (LUSH) further consolidates and synergises new and existing green initiatives, and sees the collaborative integration of urban and landscaping policies driven by the Urban Redevelopment Authority and the National Parks Board respectively.

Such policies balance the real estate economics of maximising sellable area for the benefit of the developer with the more civic imperative of creating places that can enhance the quality of life of the individual and society in general. It also ameliorates the risk of the former (private) interests outweighing the latter (public) interests – an issue that has historically seen the developer reduce recreational space to the detriment of the urban dweller and paradoxically to the long-term real estate value.

Figure 59 (top–bottom): *NTUC*, Singapore: an example of how at least 60% of the area of the skycourt should be kept open with low walls

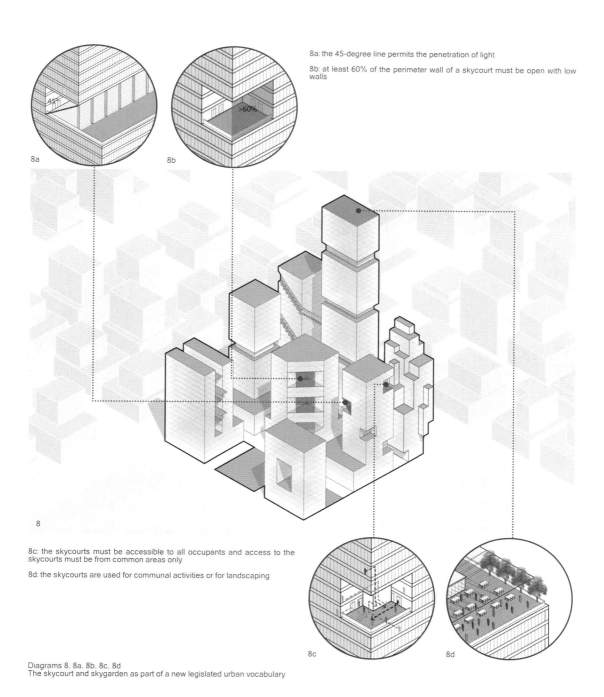

8a: the 45-degree line permits the penetration of light

8b: at least 60% of the perimeter wall of a skycourt must be open with low walls

8a

8b

8

8c: the skycourts must be accessible to all occupants and access to the skycourts must be from common areas only

8d: the skycourts are used for communal activities or for landscaping

8c

8d

Diagrams 8, 8a, 8b, 8c, 8d
The skycourt and skygarden as part of a new legislated urban vocabulary

Global case studies

Completed projects | 74
Under construction | 116
On the drawing board | 158
Future vision | 200

3. Global case studies

3.1 Completed projects

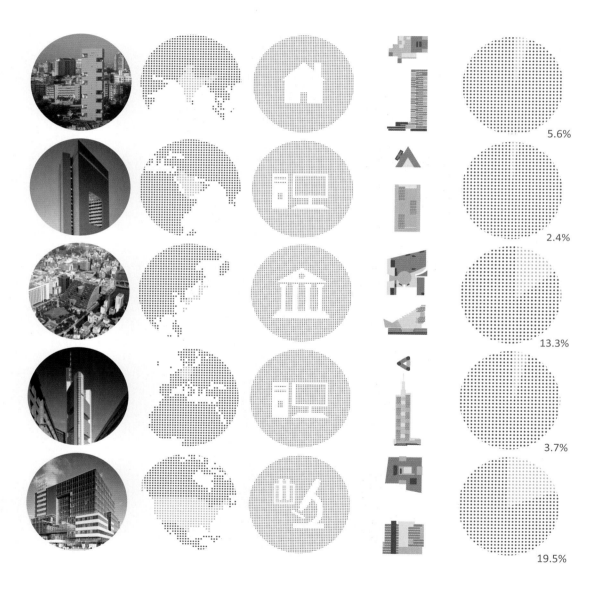

5.6%

2.4%

13.3%

3.7%

19.5%

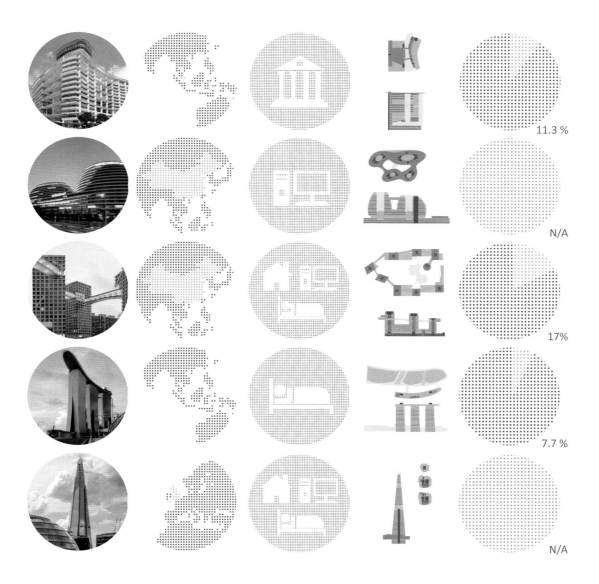

11.3 %

N/A

17%

7.7 %

N/A

Kanchanjunga

Architect	Charles Correa Associates
Location	Mumbai, India
Date	1983
Height	84 m | 32 storeys
GFA	19,960 sqm
Sector	Residential

Gross skygarden/skycourt area	1,020 sqm
Number of skygardens/skycourts	32
% of skygardens/skycourts to built-up area	5.6%

'In Bombay a building has to be oriented east–west to catch the prevailing sea-breeze. But these unfortunately are also the directions of the hot sun and the heavy monsoon rains. The old bungalows solved these problems by wrapping a protective layer of verandahs around the main living areas. Kanchanjunga, an attempt to apply these principles to a high-rise building, is a condominium of 32 luxury apartments.'

—Charles Correa

Kanchanjunga is a landmark residential development in Mumbai. Its orientation within its tropical setting demonstrates a hierarchical predominance of particular climatic factors over others in creating a comfortable living environment. The building has an east–west orientation that is exposed to the rising and setting sun and India's notorious monsoon season. However, the thermal mass of the façades, punctuated with deep recessed windows, provide an environmental buffer. The orientation allows the building to experience the prevailing wind coming from the Arabian Sea and reserves the best view of the city and the idyllic scenery of the harbour. As the impact of the monsoon season is common in this area, the skycourts have evolved as a solution to the issue by providing a double-height wind scoop, whilst allowing enough of a recess to provide shade and shelter from the low-angle sun. The Corbusien interlocking maisonette section also allows for natural ventilation to permeate deep inside the dwellings, which is further accentuated by the Venturi effect. Thus the design has effectively utilised the traditional strategies of bungalow planning in a high-rise residential development, with the skycourts acting as vertical reinterpretations of the traditional private courtyard spaces.*

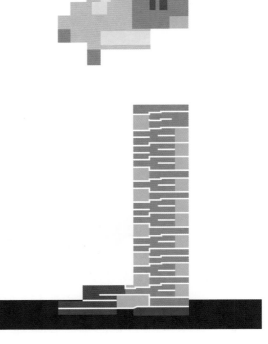

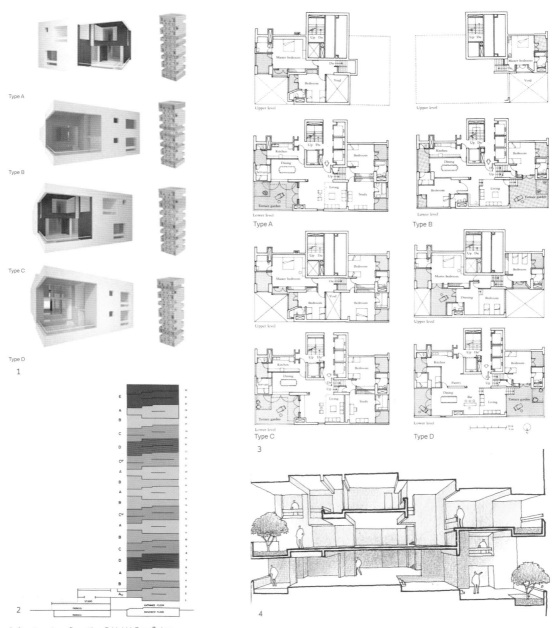

Type A

Type B

Type C

Type D

1

2

Type A

Type B

Type C

Type D

3

4

1. Apartment configuration © Hakki Can Özkan
2. Section showing arrangement of apartments © Charles Correa Associates
3. Plans of different apartment typologies © Charles Correa Associates
4. Sectional perspective © Charles Correa Associates
* With thanks to Charles Correa Associates for providing part of this text

View of *Kanchanjunga* condominium, Mumbai © Charles Correa Associates

1. View from private terrace © Charles Correa Associates
2. Private terrace © Charles Correa Associates
3. Skycourt as a traditional private courtyard space © Charles Correa Associates
4. Skycourts are positioned to optimise air flow into the residence © Charles Correa Associates

National Commercial Bank

Architect Skidmore, Owings & Merrill LLP
Location Jeddah, Saudi Arabia
Date 1983
Height 122 m | 27 storeys
GFA 57,413 sqm
Sector Commercial office

Gross skygarden/skycourt area	1,394 sqm
Number of skygardens/skycourts	3
% of skygardens/skycourts to built-up area	2.4%

'The verticality of the bank tower is interrupted by three dramatic triangular courtyards chiselled into the building's façade. Office windows open directly onto courtyards with an inward orientation typical of Islamic traditional design.'
—Skidmore, Owings & Merrill LLP

The *National Commercial Bank* is an office building located in Jeddah that forms a gateway to the commercial district on the harbour. The building's internal space provides spacious open-plan and cellular configuration offices for the 2,000 employees of the bank, along with numerous other bank-related functions. The equilateral triangle structured building was atypical of commercial structures of its time, as it sought to embrace local cultural and spatial conditions often found in Middle Eastern architecture. The sealed courtyard found commonly in the traditional architecture of the region is in this case reinterpreted as a series of vertical loggia spaces that forms gardens in the sky. These vegetated alternative social spaces provide occupants a forum for interaction as well as views of the city whilst ensuring shade on the glazed walls. The building's triangular court also extends vertically through the building in order to provide both a ventilation and light shaft. The blank exterior façades, with their absence of windows, evoke the sense of the traditional courtyard perimeter walls that turn their back on the outside world. Here, they act as an environmental buffer to the strong Middle Eastern sun, thus minimising heat gain and allowing the occupants a more shaded internal environment in which to work.*

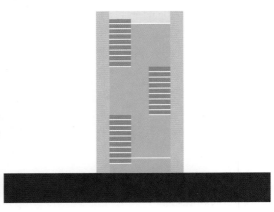

1
2
3

1. Typical plans © An Anh Nyugen
2. Typical sections © An Anh Nyugen
3. Elevations © An Anh Nyugen
* With thanks to Skidmore, Owings & Merrill LLP for providing part of this text

View of *National Commercial Bank*, Jeddah © Aga Khan Award for Architecture/Skidmore, Owings & Merrill

1. View of exterior façade from street level © Aga Khan Award for Architecture/Pascal Maréchaux
2. Worm's eye view from garden level © Aga Khan Award for Architecture/Pascal Maréchaux
3. Downward view into atrium space © Aga Khan Award for Architecture/Pascal Maréchaux
4. Exterior view © Aga Khan Award for Architecture/Skidmore, Owings & Merrill

ACROS Fukuoka Prefectural International Hall

Architect	Emilio Ambasz & Associates
Location	Fukuoka, Japan
Date	1991
Height	60 m	15 storeys
GFA	97,252 sqm
Sector	Commercial office + institutional

Gross skygarden/skycourt area	13,000 sqm
Number of skygardens/skycourts	16
% of skygardens/skycourts to built-up area	13.3%

'Each terrace floor contains an array of gardens for meditation, relaxation, and escape from the congestion of the city, while the top terrace becomes a grand belvedere, providing an incomparable view of the bay of Fukuoka and the surrounding mountains.'

—Emilio Ambasz

The *ACROS Building* is a commercial office-led, mixed-use development located in Fukuoka. The building accommodates an exhibition hall, a museum, a theatre, conference facilities, government and private offices, a parking lot and retail spaces. It was constructed on the last remaining green space in the city centre, thus necessitating the design to preserve the greenery as much as possible, whilst maintaining the development. The design effectively addresses a common urban problem – the optimisation of the buildable site area balanced with the public's need for open green space. The design fulfils both in one structure by creating an innovative agro-urban model that utilises a diagonal plane of greenery that contains some 35,000 plants representing 76 species. It also provides an opportunity to enhance the local bio-diversity by creating a home for insects, invertebrates and birds. The idea of nature is further heightened as the vegetation adopted represents the changes of the four seasons. The terraced skygardens that climb the full height of the building also provide an array of social spaces for meditation, relaxation and a welcome escape from the congestion of the city. As a result of the skycourts and their green roofs, less energy is consumed by the building as it maintains a more constant temperature inside.*

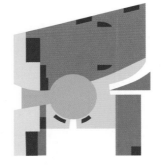

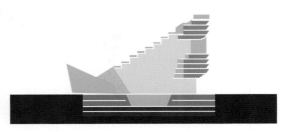

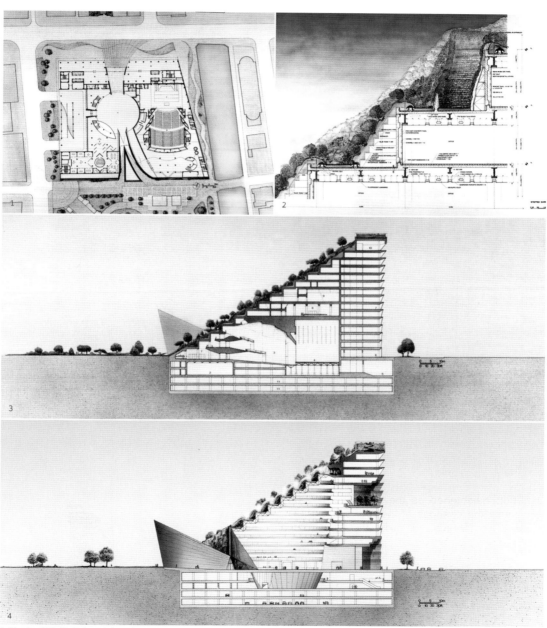

1. Site plan © Emilio Ambasz & Associates
2. Rendered section illustrating building and integrated landscape systems © Emilio Ambasz & Associates
3. Section through main auditorium space © Emilio Ambasz & Associates
4. Section showing typical floor levels © Emilio Ambasz & Associates
* With thanks to Emilio Ambasz & Associates for providing part of this text

Aerial view of *ACROS Building*, Fukuoka © Hiromi Watanabe. Courtesy of Emilio Ambasz & Associates

1. View from rooftop garden © Hiromi Watanabe, Courtesy of Emilio Ambasz & Associates
2. Relationship between architecture and greenery © Hiromi Watanabe, Courtesy of Emilio Ambasz & Associates
3. Aerial view © Hiromi Watanabe, Courtesy of Emilio Ambasz & Associates
4. View of greenery from adjacent park © Hiromi Watanabe, Courtesy of Emilio Ambasz & Associates

Commerzbank

Architect	Foster + Partners
Location	Frankfurt, Germany
Date	1997
Height	298 m | 53 storeys
GFA	120,736 sqm
Sector	Commercial office

Gross skygarden/skycourt area	4,500 sqm
Number of skygardens/skycourts	10
% of skygardens/skycourts to built-up area	3.7%

'The vertical atrium space and gardens are also part of a unique system of natural ventilation, which, for most of the year, allows the building's users to open windows in the outside wall for fresh air. This is one of the energy-saving concepts of the design.'

—Norman Foster

Commerzbank is an environmentally responsive office building located in central Frankfurt and is one of the tallest buildings in Europe. The equilateral triangle form of the building, with a central triangular atrium, embraces large skycourts on nine different levels that open up at one of the three sides. These apertures rotate every four storeys through the height of the building and offer the environmental benefit of allowing more natural light into the floor plates, thus reducing the need for artificial lighting. They also allow ventilation through the atrium, which is divided into sections, whilst not depriving the view of the city or the skycourts from the offices. The skycourts' gardens provide numerous functions and advantages that differentiate themselves from other urban working environments. They form a buffer zone of insulation between the central atrium space and the exterior space, helping provide shade by counteracting solar radiation. The incorporation of greenery into the skycourts also provides those working in the building with conducive settings for cross-departmental social interaction through chance and planned meeting, and has helped the building consume 24–30% less energy than other German office buildings.*

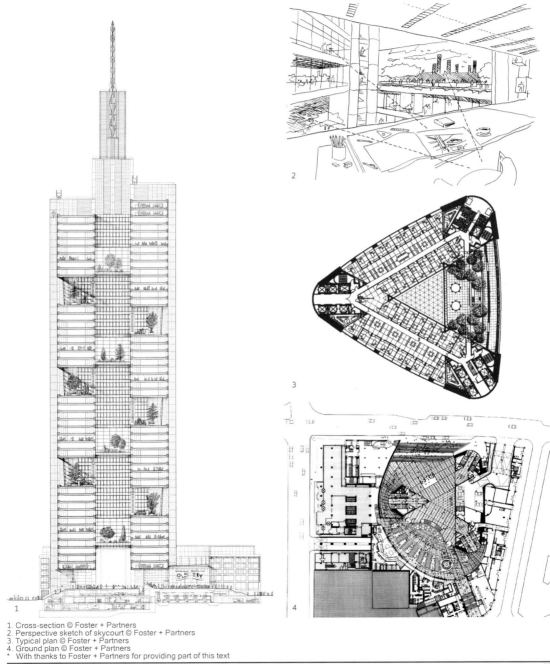

1. Cross-section © Foster + Partners
2. Perspective sketch of skycourt © Foster + Partners
3. Typical plan © Foster + Partners
4. Ground plan © Foster + Partners
* With thanks to Foster + Partners for providing part of this text

Street-level view of *Commerzbank*, Frankfurt © Ian Lambot, Courtesy of Foster + Partners

1. Interior of the skycourt © Ian Lambot
2. View from exterior into atrium space © Christian Keil
3. Social interaction occurring within the skycourt © Nigel Young. Courtesy of Foster + Partners

Genzyme Center

Architect	Behnisch Architekten
Location	Massachusetts, United States
Date	2004
Height	48.26 m	12 storeys
GFA	32,500 sqm
Sector	Research and development

Gross skygarden/skycourt area	6,325 sqm
Number of skygardens/skycourts	18
% of skygardens/skycourts to built-up area	19.5%

'The creation of different internal courtyards and gardens was fundamental to our holistic design approach. The gardens are part of the energy concept and are essential elements regarding internal communication. Our intention was to stimulate the interaction of people by creating informal meeting spaces and therefore provide a dynamic working environment.'

–Stefan Behnisch

The *Genzyme Center* is a medical/pharmaceutical research centre located on a former brownfield site in Cambridge, Massachusetts. With a gross floor area of 32,500 square metres, the office building accommodates over 900 employees. The building's interior is organised like a vertical city, with individual workspaces that function as 'dwellings' organised around generous public areas that include a library, conference facilities and a café, extending over the full height of the atrium. There are 18 different gardens that punctuate the building, each providing a place for people to meet, communicate and engage within the overall programme of the building. According to Stefan Behnisch, architect of the Center, 'the atrium links the various areas of the building, vertically and horizontally. Open stairs at the perimeter of the atrium provide connections, places and paths through the gardens and around the atrium. They are part of a "boulevard", which starts on the ground floor, amongst trees and water, and proceeds upwards. Along this vertical "boulevard", neighbourhoods with open workstations and separate offices with operable windows are developed. Workstations and interior spaces are for the most part naturally illuminated through re-directional blinds'.*

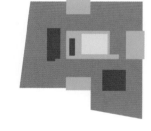

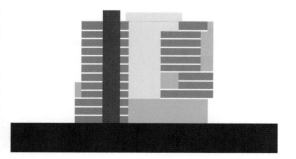

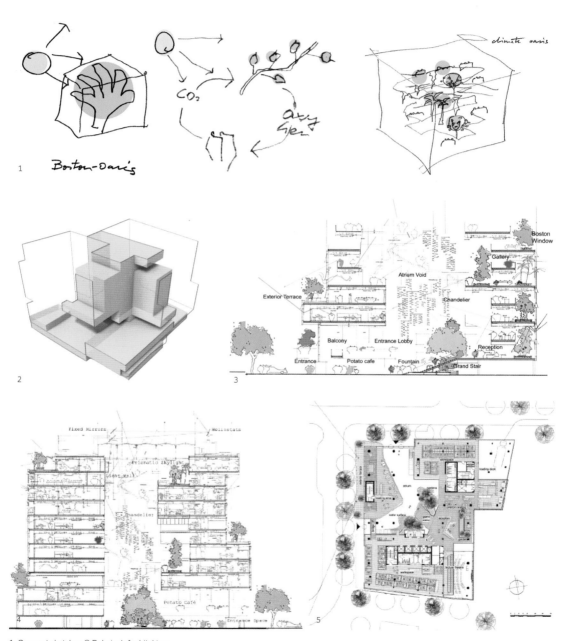

1. Concept sketches © Behnisch Architekten
2. Massing study © Behnisch Architekten
3. Sequence of gardens © Behnisch Architekten
4. Building section showing gardens, main atrium space, and Building site plan © Behnisch Architekten
* With thanks to Behnisch Architekten for providing part of this text

Street view of the *Genzyme Center*, Boston © Anton Grassi. Courtesy of Behnisch Architekten

1. Panorama of interior space © Behnisch Architekten
2. Natural light flooding atrium space © Genzyme Corporation. Courtesy of Behnisch Architekten
3. Diverse architectural landscape providing areas for social interaction © Behnisch Architekten
4. Grand stair in atrium leading to reception space © Anton Grassi. Courtesy of Behnisch Architekten

Singapore National Library

Architect	T. R. Hamzah & Yeang Sdn Bhd
Location	Bugis, Singapore
Date	2005
Height	102.8 m	16 storeys
GFA	55,565 sqm
Sector	Civic and institutional

Gross skygarden/skycourt area	6,300 sqm
Number of skygardens/skycourts	14
% of skygardens/skycourts to built-up area	11.3%

'Over 6,300 sqm of space has been designated as "green space" throughout the library which creates urban "skycourts" providing a positive psychological effect on building users and improving the general working environment.'
—T. R. Hamzah & Yeang Sdn Bhd

The *Singapore National Library* is located in the urban entertainment district of Singapore. The design consists of a curvilinear block that houses the multi-media and community-related programmes, and a rectangular block that houses the reference collection. Both are interlinked by a series of skybridges that traverse a central atrium void that extends through the centre of the blocks from the public plaza below. The plaza can hold up to up to 900 people for various cultural events and is supported by a series of skycourt spaces and skygardens that offer similar opportunities for the general public to enjoy over the height of the building. In total, over 8,000 square metres (or 10% of the total gross floor area) is designated as green space. Of the 14 skycourts and skygardens, there are two main areas situated on the fifth and tenth floors. The former is known as the Courtyard – a single-sided skycourt that is adjacent to the study lounge and provides an opportunity for group working conducive to student interaction. The latter is the Retreat – a wellness garden with a foot reflexology path and an abundance of flora and fauna that promotes quiet contemplation. Coupled with the myriad green terraced spaces, the overall vertical landscape strategy seeks to enhance bio-diversity as well as the user experience.*

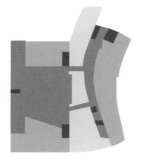

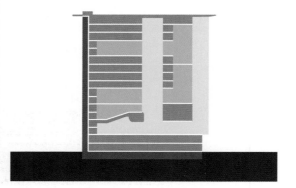

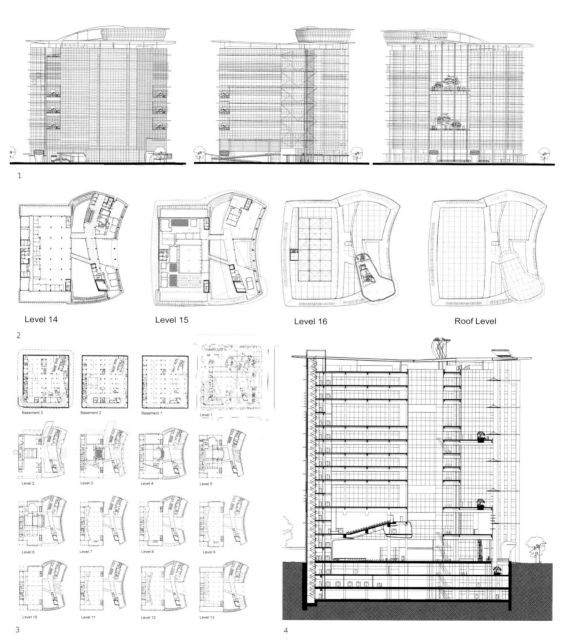

Level 14   Level 15   Level 16   Roof Level

2

Basement 3   Basement 2   Basement 1   Level 1

Level 2   Level 3   Level 4   Level 5

Level 6   Level 7   Level 8   Level 9

Level 10   Level 11   Level 12   Level 13

3

4

1. Building exterior © T. R. Hamzah & Yeang Sdn Bhd
2. Upper-level floor plans © T. R. Hamzah & Yeang Sdn Bhd
3. Floor plan series © T. R. Hamzah & Yeang Sdn Bhd
4. Building section © T. R. Hamzah & Yeang Sdn Bhd
*   With thanks to T. R. Hamzah & Yeang Sdn Bhd for providing part of this text

Street view of *National Library*, Singapore © T. R. Hamzah & Yeang Sdn Bhd

1. Worm's eye view into atrium space © T. R. Hamzah & Yeang Sdn Bhd
2. View of skycourt space from the interior © T. R. Hamzah & Yeang Sdn Bhd
3. Skycourt space © T. R. Hamzah & Yeang Sdn Bhd
4. View of planting along circulation corridor © T. R. Hamzah & Yeang Sdn Bhd

Galaxy SOHO

Architect	Zaha Hadid Architects
Location	Beijing, China
Date	2012
Height	67 m	15 storeys
GFA	332,857 sqm
Sector	Commercial office + retail

Gross skygarden/skycourt area	Confidential
Number of skygardens/skycourts	10
% of skygardens/skycourts to built-up area	Confidential

'Shifting plateaus within the design impact upon each other to generate a deep sense of immersion and envelopment. As users enter deeper into the building, they discover intimate spaces that follow the same coherent formal logic of continuous curvelinearity.'

–Zaha Hadid Architects

Galaxy SOHO is a mixed-use development in Beijing that takes its design cue from ancient Chinese traditions and has been developed through a parametric design approach that gives the development its unique fluid form. The 330,000 square metre development comprises public retail and entertainment facilities at the lowest levels. The levels immediately above provide workspaces for clusters of innovative businesses, whilst the top of the building is dedicated to bars, restaurants and cafés that offer views of the city. Notions of the traditional Chinese courtyards and terraced rice fields are woven together through multiple flowing plateaus that connect the four main volumes that resemble hills. The composition forms a new urban landscape. The separate volumes have their own atrium and cores, but merge together at various levels, providing shaded outdoor plateaus and internal spaces with dramatic views. The shifting and moving plateaus shift multiple levels into each other's view forming a deep sense of envelopment and immersion. The result is a multi-layering of social spaces that permits an ease of movement as well as heightened chances of spontaneous meeting and social interaction.*

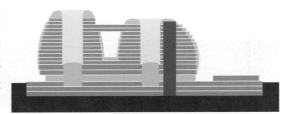

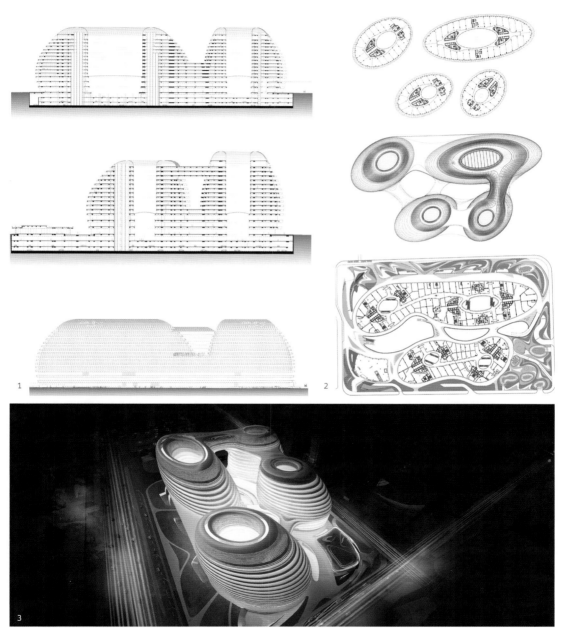

1. Cross-sections and exterior elevation © Zaha Hadid Architects
2. Building plans © Zaha Hadid Architects
3. Exterior rendering of architectural model © Zaha Hadid Architects
* With thanks to Zaha Hadid Architects for providing part of this text

Street view of *Galaxy SOHO*, Beijing © Erin O'Hara

1. Skybridges link buildings and create alternative avenues of circulation © Hufton + Crow. Courtesy of Zaha Hadid Architects
2. View of sheltered social space under linking bridge © Hufton + Crow. Courtesy of Zaha Hadid Architects
3. View of plaza © Hufton + Crow. Courtesy of Zaha Hadid Architects
4. View of broad walks in the sky © Hufton + Crow. Courtesy of Zaha Hadid Architects

Linked Hybrid

Architect	Steven Holl Architects
Location	Beijing, China
Date	2009
Height	68 m	21 storeys
GFA	221,426 sqm
Sector	Commercial office + retail + residential

Gross skygarden/skycourt area	37,642 sqm
Number of skygardens/skycourts	12
% of skygardens/skycourts to built-up area	17%

'In addition to apartments, the complex includes public, commercial, and recreational facilities as well as a hotel and school. With sitelines around, over, and through multifaceted spatial layers, this "city within a city" has as one of its central aims the concept of public space within an urban environment, and can support all the activities and programs for the daily lives of over 2,500 inhabitants.'

–Steven Holl Architects

The *Linked Hybrid* is a residential-led mixed-use development adjacent to the old city wall of Beijing. The eight towers are linked via a 20th-storey ring of skybridges that include sports facilities, education facilities, bookshops, cafés, exhibition space, and healthcare, postal and management services. These facilities support, amongst other things, 644 residential units, and provide a heightened opportunity for chance meetings amongst its residents. The design challenges pre-conceived notions of private urban spaces associated with mixed developments by vertically extrapolating them into this public sky-loop. The result is a three-dimensional urban space that encourages 24-hour interaction with others through public spaces that are activated by the commercial, residential, educational and recreational activities. The building further offers a number of open passages for visitors as well as residents to walk through, thus mitigating the sense of isolation normally associated with high-rise living. It has become one of the largest green residential projects in the world, with public skygardens, private skycourts and skygardens that connect to the penthouses.*

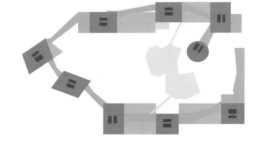

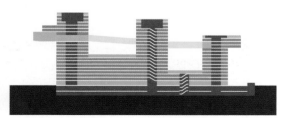

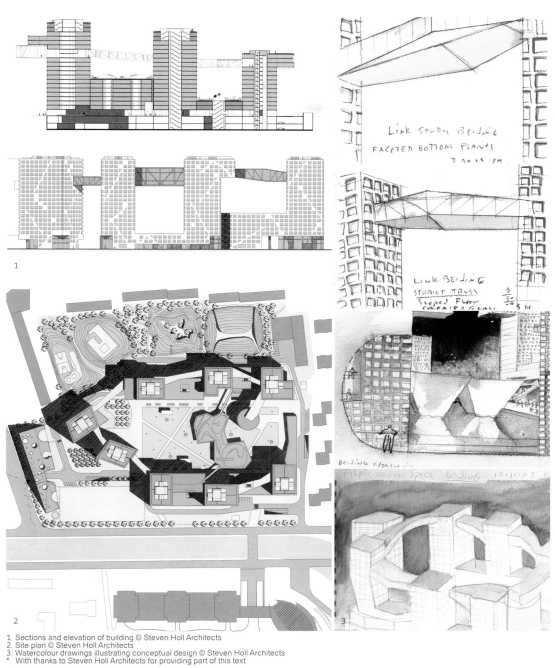

1. Sections and elevation of building © Steven Holl Architects
2. Site plan © Steven Holl Architects
3. Watercolour drawings illustrating conceptual design © Steven Holl Architects
* With thanks to Steven Holl Architects for providing part of this text

Podium view of *Linked Hybrid*, Beijing © Shu He. Courtesy of Steven Holl Architects

1. View of skybridges and roof gardens © Shu He. Courtesy of Steven Holl Architects
2. Skybridges as links between buildings © Iwan Baan. Courtesy of Steven Holl Architects
3. Auditorium space within skybridge © Shu He. Courtesy of Steven Holl Architects

Marina Bay Sands

Architect	Moshe Safdie / Safdie Architects
Location	Marina Bay, Singapore
Date	2010
Height	195 m	57 storeys
GFA	154,938 sqm
Sector	Hospitality

Gross skygarden/skycourt area	12,000 sqm
Number of skygardens/skycourts	1
% of skygardens/skycourts to built-up area	7.7%

'A series of layered gardens provide ample green space throughout Marina Bay Sands, extending the tropical garden landscape from Marina City Park towards the Bayfront. The landscape network reinforces urban connections with the resort's surroundings and every level of the district has green space that is accessible to the public.'

–Safdie Architects

The *Marina Bay Sands* is an integrated resort in Singapore that comprises a multitude of entertainment and leisure activities that includes the Sands casino. It is set within a new urban place that integrates a waterfront promenade, multi-level retail arcade, an iconic museum and a series of layered gardens that provide green space throughout Marina Bay Sands' masterplan towards the bayfront. Central to the landscape design is the 1.2 hectare skypark, which forms the urban termination of the adjacent *Gardens by the Bay*. The skypark, which includes 250 trees and 650 plants, is able to accommodate up to 3,900 people, and crowns the three prominent hotel towers that stand at 57 storeys tall. The skypark, standing at 191 metres above the ground, is the world's largest public cantilever and contains the longest (at 146 metres) pool set amongst a lush tropical landscape setting. It also includes a number of rooftop bars and restaurants positioned within the gardens, that have helped generate income for the skypark over and above the normal observation deck fee. Its ability to offer panoramic views of the financial and old districts of Singapore make it a popular destination with tourists and therefore an income-generating opportunity for the owner/operator.*

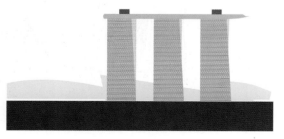

1
2
3

1. Section of tower © Safdie Architects
2. (top–bottom) Arcade floor plan. skygarden floor plan and museum section © Safdie Architects
3. Conceptual sketch of architectural form © Moshe Safdie
*   With thanks to Safdie Architects for providing part of this text

Street view of *Marina Bay Sands*, Singapore © An Anh Nguyen

1. The skygarden contains the highest swimming pool in the world © Saijel Taank
2. View from rooftop pool © Saijel Taank
3. Observation deck © Saijel Taank
4. The skycourt is densely foliated for rest and recuperation © Saijel Taank

The Shard

Architect	Renzo Piano Building Workshop
Location	London, United Kingdom
Date	2012
Height	309.6 m	95 storeys
GFA	110,000 sqm
Sector	Commercial office + residential + hospitality

Gross skygarden/skycourt area	Confidential
Number of wintergardens/skycourts	50/2
% of skygardens/skycourts to built-up area	Confidential

'In the "fractures" between the shards opening vents provide natural ventilation to winter gardens. These can be used as meeting rooms or breakout spaces in the offices and winter gardens on the residential floors. They provide a vital link with the external environment often denied in hermetically sealed buildings.'

–Renzo Piano Building Workshop

The Shard is the tallest mixed-use structure in Western Europe. Standing at 310 metres tall, it was developed by Sellar on behalf of London Bridge Quarter Ltd. The first 26 floors above the public piazza house 55,551 square metres of modern high-specification office space, with winter gardens on each floor. Restaurants and bars occupy the 31st to the 33rd floors; the five-star, 202-room Shangri La Hotel occupies the 34th to the 52nd floors, and the luxury residential apartments occupy the 53rd to the 65th floor. The View from the Shard, positioned from the 68th to the 72nd floors, completes the building. Separating the working from the living spaces is a striking three-storey skycourt on the 31st floor, designed to provide memorable views of London for visitors to the bars and restaurants. The View from the Shard also encompasses a triple-height skycourt at Level 69, and the upper-level viewing gallery at Level 72 is again triple height and also open to the elements. Renzo Piano, architect of the tower, sees The Shard 'as a small vertical town for thousands of people to work in and enjoy, and for hundreds of thousands more to visit. This is why we have included offices, restaurants, hotel, viewing galleries and residential spaces'.*

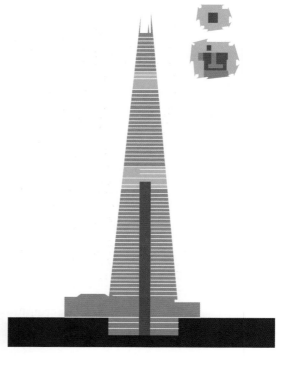

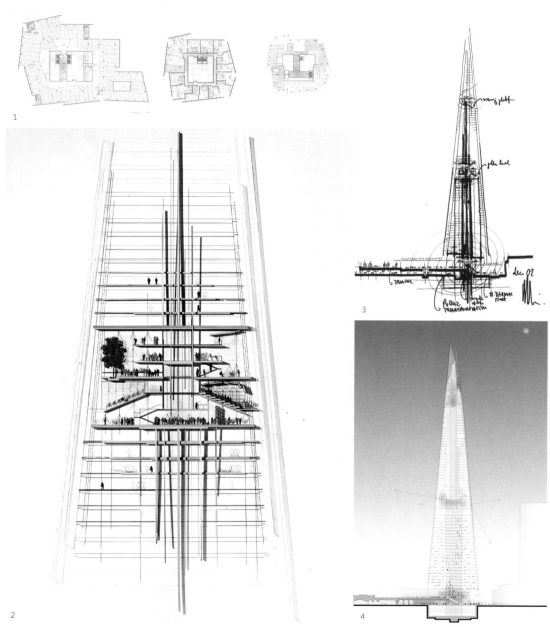

1. Plans for Levels 9, 32 and 36 © Renzo Piano Building Workshop
2. Mid-level piazza © Renzo Piano Building Workshop
3. Renzo Piano's sketch © Renzo Piano Building Workshop
4. General section © Renzo Piano Building Workshop
* With thanks to Renzo Piano Building Workshop for providing part of this text

Street view of *The Shard*, London © Simon Jenkins

1. Interior view from restaurant © Sellar
2. The View from the Shard © Sellar
3. London Bridge Station © Michel Denancé. Courtesy of Renzo Piano Building Workshop

3.2 Under construction

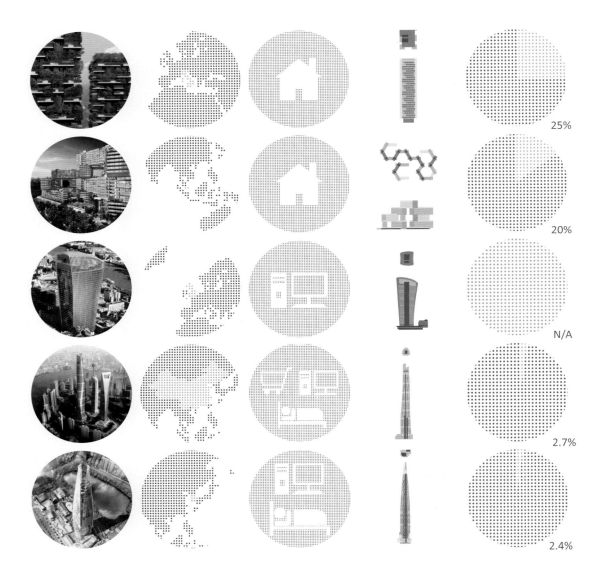

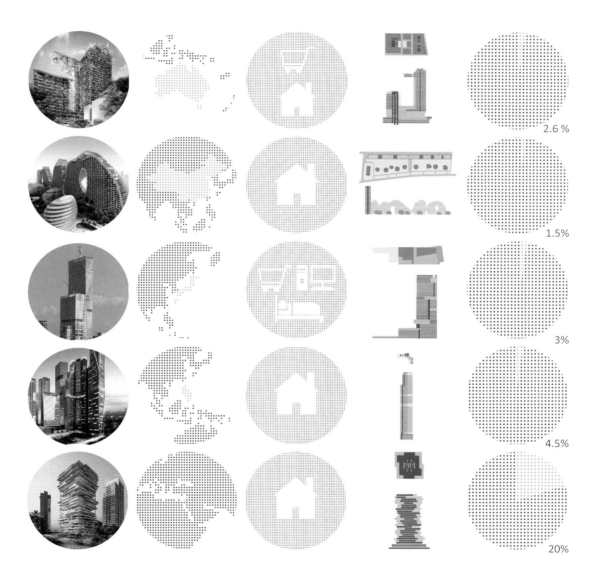

2.6 %

1.5%

3%

4.5%

20%

Bosco Verticale

Architect	Boeri Studio (Stefano Boeri, Gianandrea Barreca, Giovanni La Varra)
Location	Milan, Italy
Date	Anticipated completion: 2013
Height	110 m and 76 m | 28 and 21 storeys
GFA	40,000 sqm
Sector	Residential

Gross skygarden/skycourt area	10,000 sqm
Number of skygardens/skycourts	132
% of skygardens/skycourts to built-up area	25%

'In the same way that green elements are increasingly often involved in the redesign of the public spaces of our cities, plants are now becoming materials and elements in a rethinking of the façade as the building's principal infrastructure, where performance must be optimized in terms of energy saving.'
—Boeri Studio

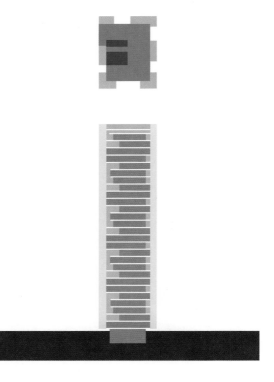

The *Bosco Verticale*, or 'Vertical Forest', is a model for urban reforestation that sets forth a strategy to replenish greenery within contemporary European cities. The two residential towers of 110 and 76 metres in height will be realised in the centre of Milan, on the edge of the Isola neighbourhood. The design will house a total of 900 trees (each measuring 3, 6 or 9 metres tall) apart from a wide range of shrubs and floral plants to effectively create a vertical forest. The use of plants and vegetation will assist in balancing the microclimate and will filter the dust particles in the urban environment. Each apartment has trees provided on every balcony that will be able to respond to the city's changing seasons. In the summer they will provide shade, and in the winter the bare trees will allow sunlight to penetrate through the spaces, all the while filtering the city's pollution. The diversity of the plants absorb carbon dioxide and dust particles as well as enhance humidity and reduce ambient temperatures. Furthermore, the plants will produce oxygen and protect from radiation and acoustic pollution. As a result, the planting strategies seek to not only save energy but also enhance the quality of living, especially given the correlation between planting and the proven socio-physiological benefits it has on people.*

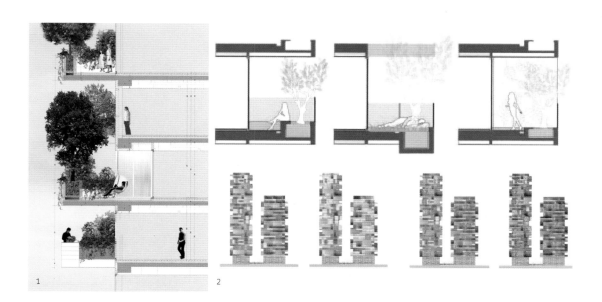

1   2

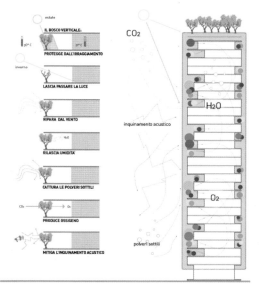

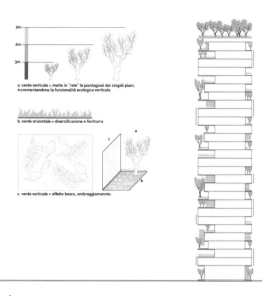

3   4

1. Human interaction with greenery © Boeri Studio
2. Effects of the seasons on the buildings' appearance © Boeri Studio
3. Environmental strategies © Boeri Studio
4. Planting typologies © Boeri Studio
*   With thanks to Boeri Studio for providing part of this text

Construction of *Bosco Verticale*. Milan © Marco Garofalo. Courtesy of Boeri Studio

1. Rendering of building façade © Boeri Studio
2. Lifting of trees into building © Marco Garofalo. Courtesy of Boeri Studio
3. Placing of trees into planters © Marco Garofalo. Courtesy of Boeri Studio
4. View of skycourts cladding residential units © Boeri Studio

The Interlace

Architect	OMA
Location	Singapore
Date	Anticipated completion: 2014
Height	83 m | 24 storeys
GFA	170,000 sqm
Sector	Residential

Gross skygarden/skycourt area	34,141 sqm
Number of skygardens/skycourts	132
% of skygardens/skycourts to built-up area	20%

'The Interlace, one of the largest and most ambitious residential developments in Singapore, presents a radically new approach to contemporary living in a tropical environment. Instead of creating a cluster of isolated, vertical towers – the default typology of residential developments in Singapore – the design proposes an intricate network of living and social spaces integrated with the natural environment.'

—OMA

The Interlace adopts an innovative design concept that breaks away from the conventional high-rise structures of the high-density residential typology. With 170,000 square metres of built floor area, the development will provide over 1,000 residential units of varying sizes, each with unobstructed and varying views over the parks, the city and the sea. The large-scale complex takes a more expansive and interconnected approach to living through communal spaces, which are integrated into its lush surrounding greenbelt. The 31 apartment blocks, each consisting six storeys, are counterpoised and interlocked with one another to create eight large hexagonal and highly permeable courtyards, supported by nine public roof gardens, and 99 private roof gardens. The interlocking blocks create a vertical village of both shared and private outdoor spaces on multiple levels. The overall site area, totalling eight hectares, is densely foliated with lush tropical vegetation that takes place both on the ground and in the sky. The continuous landscape is also projected vertically, from the planting of green areas in open-air basement voids, through balconies and rooftop gardens. The private balconies give apartments large outdoor space and personal planting areas.*

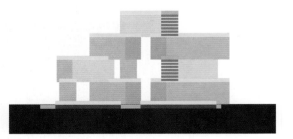

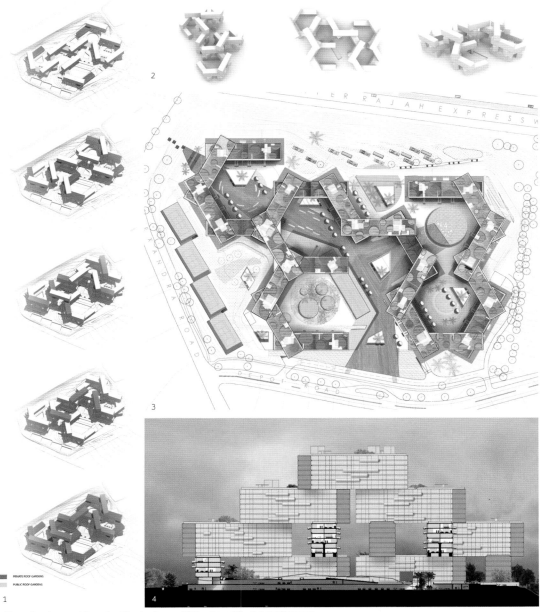

1. Skygarden placement throughout the development © Courtesy of CapitaLand Singapore
2. Massing study © Courtesy of CapitaLand Singapore
3. Site plan © Courtesy of CapitaLand Singapore
4. Site section © Courtesy of CapitaLand Singapore
* With thanks to OMA for providing part of this text

Rendering of *The Interlace*. Singapore © Courtesy of CapitaLand Singapore

1. Aerial rendering of *The Interlace* © Courtesy of CapitaLand Singapore
2. Image of bamboo garden © Courtesy of CapitaLand Singapore
3. Image of common skygarden © Courtesy of CapitaLand Singapore
4. View of the construction status. February 2013 © Courtesy of CapitaLand Singapore

20 Fenchurch Street

Architect	Rafael Viñoly Architects PC
Location	London, United Kingdom
Date	Anticipated completion: 2014
Height	177 m | 38 storeys
GFA	64,100 sqm
Sector	Commercial office + retail

Gross skygarden/skycourt area	Confidential
Number of skygardens/skycourts	1
% of skygardens/skycourts to built-up area	Confidential

'London today is one of the most interesting architectural laboratories in recent history. We designed 20 Fenchurch Street to respect the city's historic character, following the contour of the river and the medieval streets that bound the site, while further contributing to the evolution of the high-rise building type.'

—Raphael Viñoly Architects

20 Fenchurch Street is a mixed-use tall building in the heart of London, developed by Land Securities and Canary Wharf Group in a joint-venture partnership. The design, which has been nicknamed the 'walkie talkie' given its increasing vertical width, is designed to provide larger floor plates at height in response to tenant demands and to maximise the public realm/streetscape at the ground level. The building is orientated to minimise environmental impact, which is further protected by vertical louvres that provide sun shading to the east and west elevations that organically wrap up and over the roof and skygarden. The skygarden tops the building with a publicly accessible skyscraper observation deck – a dramatic, multi-storey space that features landscaping, cafés and expansive 360-degree views of the city. Accessed through a separate lobby and dedicated elevators, the skygarden will be open to the public free of charge, and is a further example of the 'public good' that skygardens can offer civil society within dense urban habitats.*

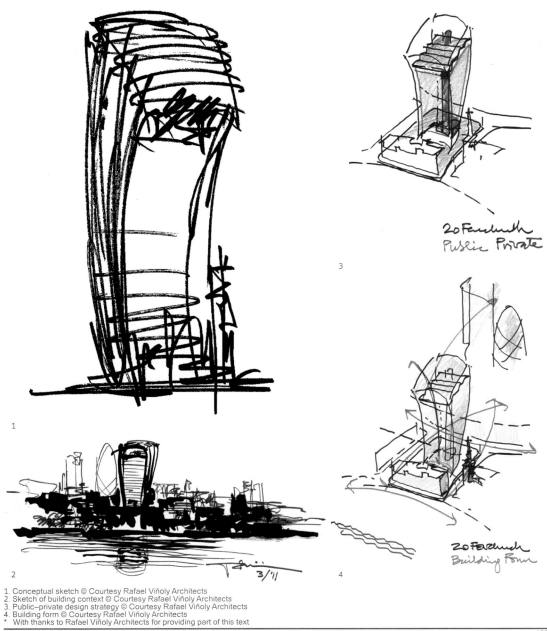

20 Fenchurch
Public Private

3

20 FENCHURCH
Building Form

1

2   3/'11   4

1. Conceptual sketch © Courtesy Rafael Viñoly Architects
2. Sketch of building context © Courtesy Rafael Viñoly Architects
3. Public–private design strategy © Courtesy Rafael Viñoly Architects
4. Building form © Courtesy Rafael Viñoly Architects
*   With thanks to Rafael Viñoly Architects for providing part of this text

Rendering of *20 Fenchurch Street*, London © Land Securities and Canary Wharf Group

1. Skygarden © Land Securities and Canary Wharf Group
2. View from the skygarden © Land Securities and Canary Wharf Group
3. Building construction status © Land Securities and Canary Wharf Group

Shanghai Tower

Architect	Gensler
Location	Shanghai, China
Date	Anticipated completion: 2014
Height	632 m	121 storeys
GFA	574,000 sqm
Sector	Commercial office + hospitality + retail

Gross skygarden/skycourt area	15,268 sqm
Number of skygardens/skycourts	21
% of skygardens/skycourts to built-up area	2.7%

'With its emphasis on public space and its shops, restaurants, and other urban amenities strategically located at the floors with public atria, Shanghai Tower envisions a new way of inhabiting super-tall towers. Each of the building's neighborhoods rises from a "sky lobby" at its base – a light-filled garden atrium that creates a sense of community and supports daily life. The entire tower will have an inside-outside transparency and is the only super-highrise building wrapped in public spaces and sky courts.'

–Gensler

The *Shanghai Tower* is a mixed-use tower situated in the heart of the Shanghai financial district. The building incorporates 121 floors, which will make it the second tallest building in the world when completed in 2014, and expects an estimated occupancy of 16,000 people. Comprising of office, hospitality, retail and entertainment functions, the tall building was conceived as a vertical city. The façade design seeks to reduce wind loads on the building by up to 24%, resulting in fewer construction materials and a reduction in steel needed – thus saving an estimated US $58 million in material costs. The tower embraces a mixed mode of power generation, which is created in part by wind turbines that are estimated to be able to generate up to 1,190,000 kWh of supplementary electricity per year. The analogy to a vertical city is taken further by the separation of the tower into nine zones, which incorporate skycourts for visitors to enjoy. Each space has its own atrium with a series of stepped planted skycourts, cafés, restaurants and retail space, which will allow a 360-degree view of the city. The skycourts serve much as plazas and squares do, bringing people together throughout the day. Each one harkens back to the city's historic open courtyards, which combine indoor/outdoor landscaped settings.*

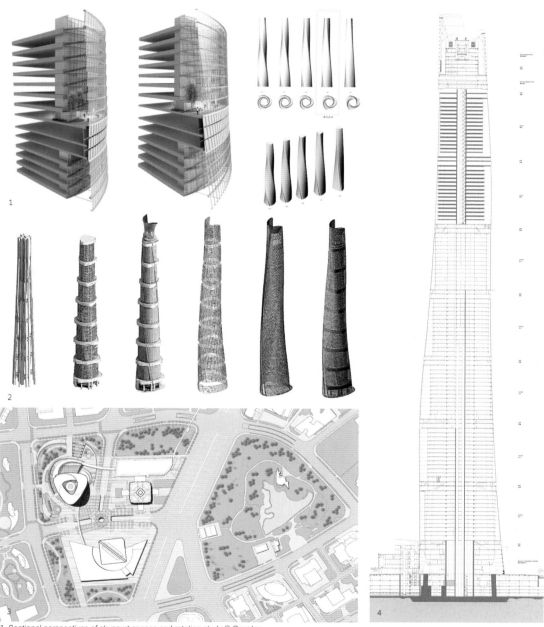

1. Sectional perspectives of skycourt spaces and rotation study © Gensler
2. Build up from structure to façade © Gensler
3. Site plan © Gensler
4. Building section © Gensler
* With thanks to Gensler for providing part of this text

Rendering of the *Shanghai Tower*, Shanghai © Gensler

1. Interior perspectives of skycourt spaces © Gensler
2. Rendered site plan © Gensler
3. Current construction status of the tower © Gensler

Lotte Tower

Architect	Kohn Pedersen Fox Associates
Location	Seoul, South Korea
Date	Anticipated completion: 2015
Height	555 m	123 storeys
GFA	303,591 sqm
Sector	Commercial office + hospitality

Gross skygarden/skycourt area	7,195 sqm
Number of skygardens/skycourts	4
% of skygardens/skycourts to built-up area	2.4%

'The sky lobbies, or sky courts, are an essential part of the Lotte Tower design. The stacking of functions is so varied, and the vertical transport system needed to serve these uses is complex. These spaces are needed to orient the user groups on each arrival floor. They also relieve the pressure to provide for a long list of spaces at the ground floor. The lower levels of the tower are already packed with arrival spaces, security sequences, retail, elevator traffic, and the like.'

—Kohn Pedersen Fox

Lotte Tower is a 555 metre, 123-storey mixed-use building in Seoul. The 'vertical city' programme starts with the first seven floors being dedicated to retail in order to take advantage of the large floor plate area, and a bridge connection to a large retail/cultural building. Floors 13 to 38 are dedicated to office space, Floors 42 to 71 house officetel space, and Floors 76 to 101 are earmarked to contain a six-star luxury hotel. The remaining upper floors of the 123-storey tower are allotted for private offices, as well as for public use and entertainment facilities, which include the observation deck and rooftop café. The tower will stand out from the city's rugged mountainous topography as a slender tapered cone, and to this end, will become a new landmark for the city skyline when completed in 2015. Korea's long history of ceramic, porcelain and calligraphic artistry was a source of initial inspiration for the design of the tower. The tower's uninterrupted curvature and gentle tapered form is reflective of such Korean artistry, and the seam that runs from top to bottom of the structure gestures towards the old centre of the city.*

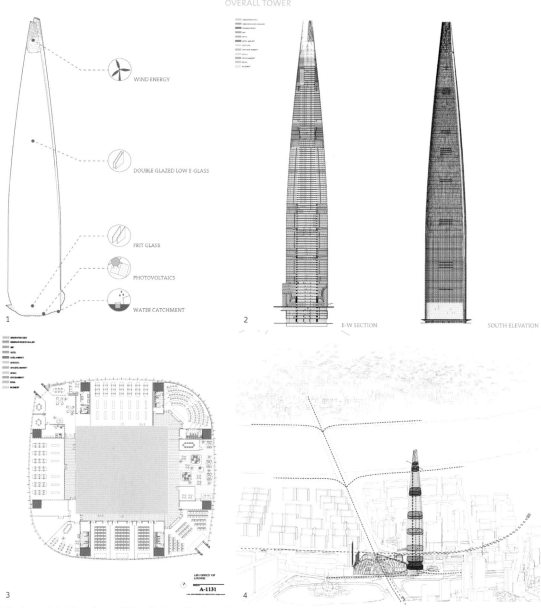

OVERALL TOWER

WIND ENERGY

DOUBLE GLAZED LOW E-GLASS

FRIT GLASS

PHOTOVOLTAICS

WATER CATCHMENT

1

2

E-W SECTION

SOUTH ELEVATION

3

4

1. Environmental strategy diagram © Kohn Pedersen Fox Associates
2. Building section and elevation © Kohn Pedersen Fox Associates
3. Typical plan © Kohn Pedersen Fox Associates
4. Movement strategy diagram © Kohn Pedersen Fox Associates
* With thanks to Kohn Pedersen Fox Associates for providing part of this text

Rendering of *Lotte Tower*, Seoul © Kohn Pedersen Fox Associates

1. VIP lounge © Kohn Pedersen Fox Associates
2. *Lotte Tower* under construction © Kohn Pedersen Fox Associates
3. Top of tower © Kohn Pedersen Fox Associates
4. Observation deck © Kohn Pedersen Fox Associates

One Central Park

Architect	Ateliers Jean Nouvel
Location	Sydney, Australia
Date	Anticipated completion: 2015
Height	80 m and 165 m| 16 and 33 storeys
GFA	250,000 sqm
Sector	Residential + retail

Gross skygarden/skycourt area	6,600 sqm
Number of skygardens/skycourts	2
% of skygardens/skycourts to built-up area	2.6%

'A vertical landscape designed in collaboration with French botanist and artist Patrick Blanc covers approximately 50% of the building's façade area. The landscape extends the planted are of the adjacent urban park vertically onto the building, creating an exceptional living environment for the building's residents and a powerful green icon on the Sydney skyline.'

–Ateliers Jean Nouvel

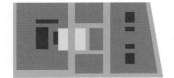

One Central Park is a residential and retail development in central Sydney on the site of a former brewery. The two residential towers, each of which being 16 and 33 storeys, will sit above a six-storey retail and recreational podium. Architect Jean Nouvel collaborated with botanist Patrick Blanc to create over 12 vertical gardens that seek to replenish the urban greenery by the installation of a green vertical forest across the façades of the towers. The vertical gardens within the two residential towers will house 250 species of Australian flowers and plants that change according to the different seasons. Vegetation and vines will step in and out of skycourt spaces, that will overflow from the building and create an ecological corridor to the ground-level park. The eastern tower features a dramatic heliostat installation, extending from the upper levels on a monumental cantilever. The heliostat incorporates an innovative system of fixed and motorised mirrored panels designed to capture sunlight and redirect it into the retail atrium and onto the landscaped terraces. At night the heliostat's integrated lighting – designed by lighting artist Yann Kersale – will theatrically and colourfully illuminate the towers.*

1. Building façade application study and architectural programme © Ateliers Jean Nouvel
2. Site plan and building section illustrating green areas © Ateliers Jean Nouvel
3. Building elevation and section © Ateliers Jean Nouvel
* With thanks to Ateliers Jean Nouvel for providing part of this text

Rendering of *One Central Park*, Sydney © Ateliers Jean Nouvel

1. External view of cantilevered skygarden with plunge pool © Frasers Property Australia and Sekisui House Australia
2. View of civic place © Ateliers Jean Nouvel
3. The lifting of the 110-tonne heliostat frame which is cantilevered 40 metres off the façade, Sydney © Frasers Property Australia and Sekisui House Australia

Fake Hills

Architect	MAD
Location	Beihai, China
Date	Anticipated completion: 2014
Height	194 m	32 storeys
GFA	492,369 sqm
Sector	Residential

Gross skygarden/skycourt area	7,195 sqm
Number of skygardens/skycourts	136
% of skygardens/skycourts to built-up area	1.5%

'A further reference point is traditional Chinese architecture's obsession with nature. Rather than setting the building in a perfect, man-made natural garden, our structure becomes the man-made natural shape itself: fake hills for the residents to live on.'
—MAD Architects

Fake Hills is a residential development located in the coastal city of Beihai, that challenges the pre-conceived notions of set-piece architectural creations (opera houses, museums, stadiums, by way of examples that are also the exceptions to the rules) caused by China's ultra-rapid urbanisation. According to the architects, the vast majority of development in China's new cities takes the form of residential schemes, often economic through standardisation to guarantee quick returns for the developer. The design concept combines two conventional structures (high-rise towers and long slabs) to create the curved outline in the form of the man-made hills. This shape can maximise the views of residents; it also builds up a close relationship with the waterfront and the land behind it. Openings cut through the structure allow sea views and sea breezes to penetrate it. The continuous platform along the roof becomes the public space for the residents, with green skygardens that form the basis in which tennis courts, swimming pools and a host of other recreational facilities can take place on top of the man-made hills.*

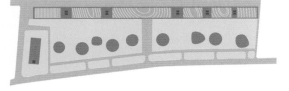

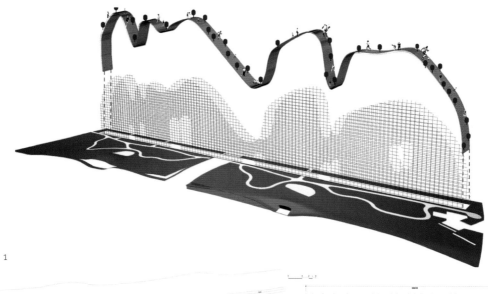

1

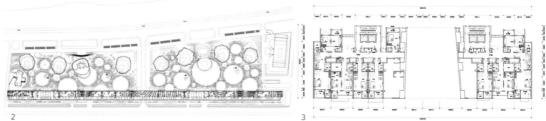

2

3

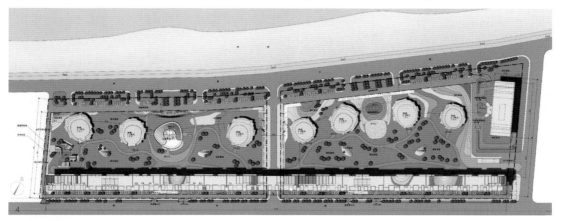

4

1. Exploded diagram of greenery © MAD Architects
2. Site plan © MAD Architects
3. Typical unit plans © MAD Architects
4. Landscaping plan © MAD Architects
* With thanks to MAD Architects for providing part of this text

Rendering of *Fake Hills*, Beihai © MAD Architects

1. Night rendering of *Fake Hills* © MAD Architects
2. Construction status © MAD Architects
3. View of construction status from ground level © MAD Architects
4. Overall view of *Fake Hills* © MAD Architects

Abeno HARUKAS

Architect	Takenaka Corporation + Pelli Clarke Pelli Architects
Location	Osaka, Japan
Date	Anticipated completion: 2014
Height	300 m | 60 storeys
GFA	306,000 sqm
Sector	Retail + commercial office + hotel + museum + observatory

Gross skygarden/skycourt area	8,752 sqm
Number of skygardens/skycourts	5
% of skygardens/skycourts to built-up area	3%

'The building features open spaces that let in natural light and air, rooftop green space, and biogas power generated by energy recovered through methane fermentation from the building's kitchen waste.'

—Kintetsu Corporation

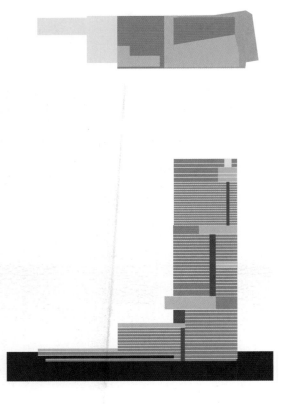

Abeno HARUKAS is a 300-metre-tall mixed-use development in Osaka, that will become the tallest building in Japan. This transit-orientated development will be one of the largest railway terminal buildings in the world, and comprises 60 storeys above the ground and five underground storeys. The vertical city will house approximately 306,000 square metres of various functions which will include a department store, museum, office, hotel and observatory. Three volumes with different footprints are shifted and stacked to admit sunlight and wind to the central core of the office space, and to create continuous steps of three-dimensional skygardens in conjunction with the adjacent Tennoji Park. The skycourts installed in each building have various expressions according to the usage and the environment. In the museum garden (80 metres above ground) a rich copse appears by mapping various vegetation of the Uemachi plateau. The evergreen trees of oak in addition to the deciduous trees, such as zelkova and maples, are also planted. Shrubs are further planted around the base of the tall trees to create the atmosphere of a copse. Bamboo grasses are planted in the skygarden (200 metres above ground and where down drafts are stronger) to evoke the sense of a mountain hillside. Oaks are planted on the 58th floor to provide guests to the observatory with a shaded environment whilst gleaning memorable views.*

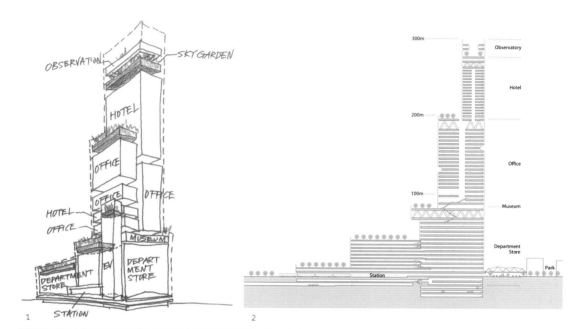

1. Sectional diagram of building © Takenaka Corporation
2. Conceptual sketch © Takenaka Corportaion
3. Aerial plan © Takenaka Corporation
* With thanks to Takenaka Corporation for providing part of this text

View of *Abeno HARUKAS*, Osaka © Takenaka Corporation

1. Rendering and construction status of the 16th-storey museum skygarden © Takenaka Corporation
2. Rendering of the 38th-storey hotel garden © Takenaka Corporation
3. Day-time, night-time and construction status of the 58th-storey skygarden © Takenaka Corporation

Gramercy Residences

Architect	Jerde Partnership Inc. + Pomeroy Studio
Location	Makati, Philippines
Date	Anticipated completion: 2013
Height	280 m	73 storeys
GFA	77,000 sqm
Sector	Residential

Gross skygarden/skycourt area	3,500 sqm
Number of skygardens/skycourts	2
% of skygardens/skycourts to built-up area	4.5%

'The curvilinear arrangement of Gramercy Park's greenery was then abstracted to define the curvilinear layouts of densely foliated green walls and the planters. Indigenous species were used to clad the walls to evoke the sense of a "hanging garden.'
–Pomeroy Studio

The *Gramercy Residences* is a high-end residential tall building that lies at the heart of Manila's central business district and will be the tallest building in the Philippines. By virtue of its 73-storey height, it also houses the tallest skycourt in the Philippines, which takes place over the 36th and 37th floors. Acknowledging the high-density nature of Manila and its lack of green space, the design intent was to recreate the Gramercy Park in Manhattan – a beautiful pocket park in the middle of the city, with mature trees and pleasant pathways in which residents can relax, exercise or engage with others. The 3,500 square metre skypark acts as a recreational social space in the sky for the building's residents and contains a host of facilities that are the first of their kind in the Philippines. In addition to lap pools, children's play areas, meeting rooms, a restaurant and bar, yoga decks and a gymnasium, it also has fully integrated water and mist features and an abundance of vertical urban greenery to create a 'hanging garden' in the sky. Part of the skypark will also be home to the tallest green wall in the country.

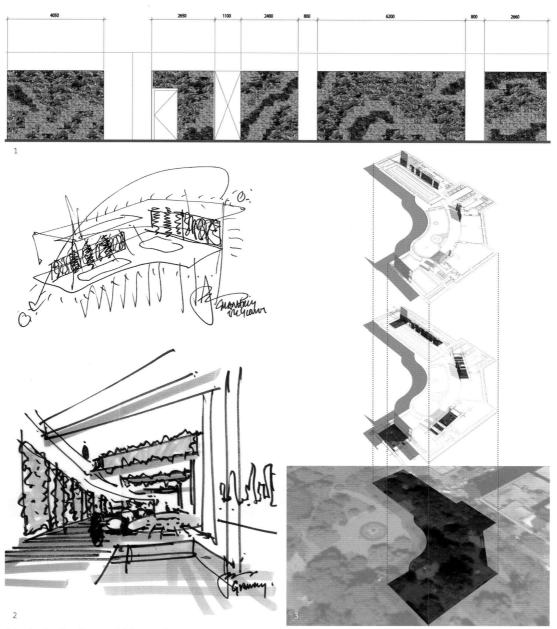

1. Interior elevation of green wall © Pomeroy Studio
2. Conceptual sketches © Pomeroy Studio
3. Conceptual development of green wall patterning © Pomeroy Studio

View of *Gramercy Residences*, Manila © Dave Calder

1. Rendering of 36th-floor skycourt © Pomeroy Studio
2. Rendering of main pool and green wall © Pomeroy Studio
3. Skygarden under construction © Tom Epperson for Century Properties

Beirut Terraces

Architect	Herzog & de Meuron
Location	Beirut, Lebanon
Date	Anticipated completion: 2015
Height	119 m	26 storeys
GFA	101,000 sqm
Sector	Residential

Gross terrace area	11,461 sqm
% of terraced area to built-up area	20%

'Five principles define the project: layers and terraces, inside and outside, vegetation, views and privacy, light and identity. The result is a vertically layered building: slabs of varying sizes allow for interplay between openness and privacy that fosters flexible living between inside and outside.'

—Herzog & de Meuron

Beirut Terraces is a high-end residential development situated in the Mina el Hosn district, Beirut's most reputable area and a place for luxury hotels, high-end fashion retailers, restaurants and historic scenery. It will be comprised of 131 single, duplex and townhouse apartments within a 119.13-metre-high structure that is characterised by a series of stratified layers that are symbolic of the layers of the city's rich and tumultuous history. The architects have structured the building on five specific principles: layers and terraces, inside and outside, vegetation, views and privacy, light and identity. The result is a vertically layered building expressed by diverse sizes of slabs which create both openness and privacy and enable flexible living between inside and outside. This allows residents to embrace nature and the outdoors through the implementation of vegetation and exterior surfaces. The differentiated structure for each individual apartment allows terraces and overhangs for light and shadow, and places for shelter and exposure. Not only do these alternating overhangs provide shadows, however; they also decrease the solar heat gains of the building and significantly distinguish the identity of the tower from its surroundings.*

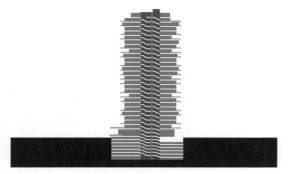

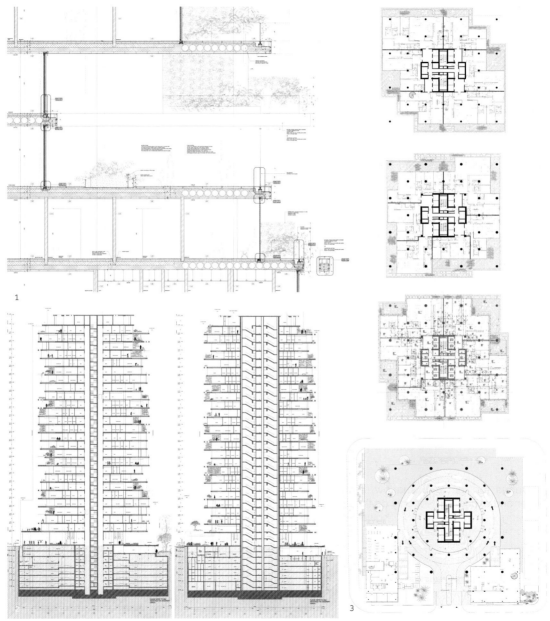

1. Façade detail section © 2012, Herzog & de Meuron Basel
2. Building sections © 2012, Herzog & de Meuron Basel
3. Ground-floor plan © 2012, Herzog & de Meuron Basel
* With thanks to Herzog & de Meuron Basel for providing part of this text

Rendering of *Beirut Terraces*, Beirut © 2012, Herzog & de Meuron Basel

1. Perspective view of terraces © 2012, Herzog & de Meuron Basel
2. View of skycourt terrace © 2012, Herzog & de Meuron Basel
3. Construction progress © 2013, Benchmark Development

3.3 On the drawing board

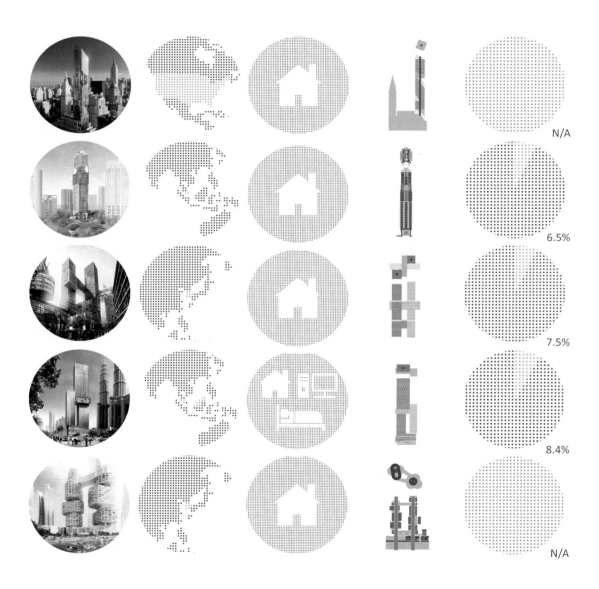

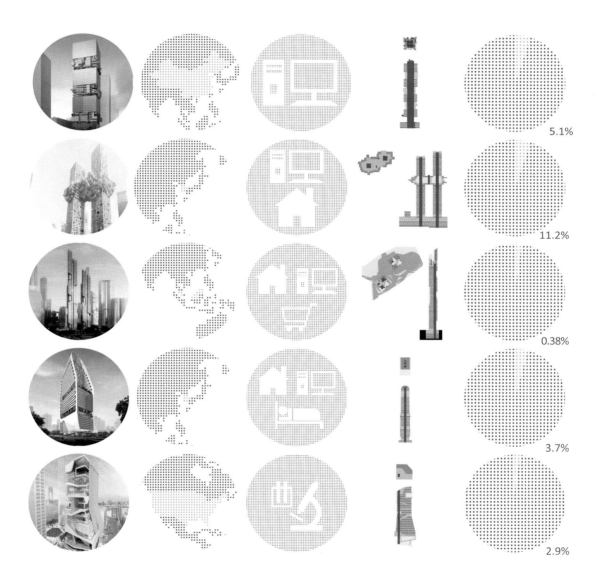

5.1%

11.2%

0.38%

3.7%

2.9%

One Madison Avenue

Architect	Studio Daniel Libeskind
Location	New York City, United States
Date	Anticipated completion: TBD
Height	284 m	54 storeys
Area	4,460 sqm
Sector	Residential

Gross skygarden/skycourt area	Confidential
Number of skygardens/skycourts	31
% of skygardens/skycourts to built-up area	Confidential

'The design features a series of spiraling gardens extending the green of Madison Square along the façade of the tower. The tower is set back from its neighbors – maintaining views and maximizing light and air. We didn't just fill up the tower, we've taken space away [from the apartments] to create the gardens, which are actually balconies tucked within the envelope. It's as if nature has come back into the city.'

–Daniel Libeskind

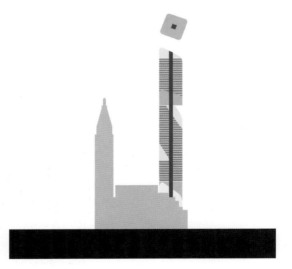

One Madison Avenue will be a 54-storey residential building in central New York. The development seeks to exploit the air rights above an existing 14-storey masonry building that is an annex for the Metropolitan Life building. The concept takes its cue from the greenery of Madison Square Park, which is adjacent to the building. This is experienced through a spiralling skygarden that slices through the extruded square footprint that defines the building form. Standing at 284 metres, it will be the tallest residential building in the city. The glass façade of the project will be interrupted by the green spaces within them that will form private recreational skycourts for the residents. Residents therefore benefit from having an outdoor connection, fresh air and a space to grow their own vegetation or plants – rare commodities given the high-density nature of the city.*

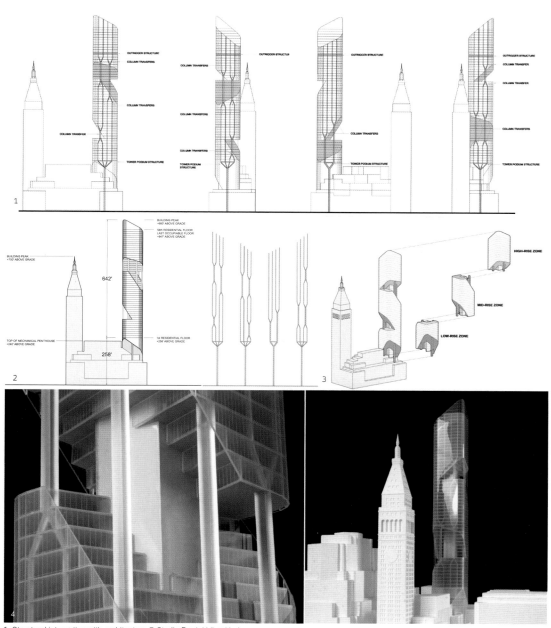

1. Structural integration with architecture © Studio Daniel Libeskind
2. Overall height and structural system © Studio Daniel Libeskind
3. Exploded zones © Studio Daniel Libeskind
4. Model images © Studio Daniel Libeskind
* With thanks to Studio Daniel Libeskind for providing part of this text

Rendering of *One Madison Avenue*. New York © Studio Daniel Libeskind

1. Detailed view of the skycourt © Studio Daniel Libeskind
2. View at night with illuminated skycourt spaces © Studio Daniel Libeskind
3. Street view © Studio Daniel Libeskind

Scotts Tower

Architect	UNStudio
Location	Singapore
Date	Anticipated completion: 2015
Height	153 m	31 storeys
GFA	18,500 sqm
Sector	Residential

Gross skygarden/skycourt area	1,194 sqm
Number of skygardens/skycourts	2
% of skygardens/skycourts to built up-area	6.5%

'Instead of the more usual means of planning a city horizontally, we have created neighborhoods in the sky – a vertical city where each zone has its own distinct identity'.
–Ben Van Berkel, UNStudio

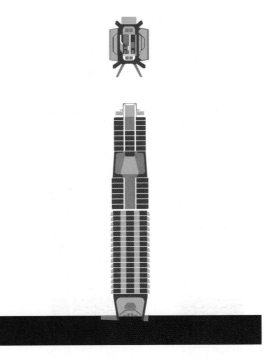

Scotts Tower is a 31-storey high-end residential tall building in the core of Singapore's luxurious shopping district, Orchard Road. The vertical city concept is interpreted in three scales: the 'city', the 'neighbourhood' and the 'home'. The three elements of the vertical city concept along with the social space areas are bound together by two gestures: the 'vertical frame' and the 'sky frames'. The vertical frame organises the tower architecturally in an urban manner. The frame affords the tower the vertical city effect by dividing the four residential clusters into different neighbourhoods. The sky frames – at the lobby (Level 1 and Level 2) and sky terrace (Level 25) – organise the recreational amenities of the tower. There is an individual identity given to the four residential clusters, which is defined through the type, scale, distribution and articulation of the outdoor space. Within the development is a green area that extends into the Scotts Tower site. This green area integrates the recreational facilities that include children's pool, dining and BBQ pavilions, the 50-metre lap pool and a gymnasium. Additionally, residences can enjoy the skycourts created by the lower and upper skyframe terraces.*

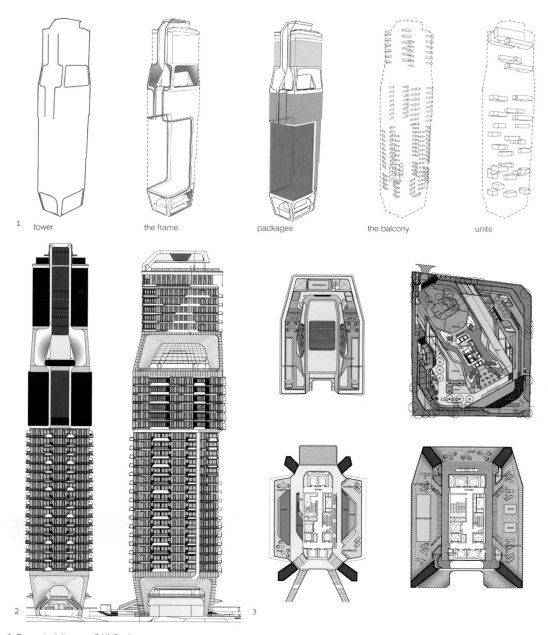

1   tower   the frame   packages   the balcony   units

1. Conceptual diagrams © UNStudio
2. East and north elevations © UNStudio
3. Plans © UNStudio
*   With thanks to UNStudio for providing part of this text

Rendering of *Scotts Tower*, Singapore © UNStudio

1. Aerial panoramic of skycourt © UNStudio
2. View of skygarden on penthouse © UNStudio
3. Pool on skycourt level © UNStudio

Cross # Towers

Architect	BIG
Location	Seoul, South Korea
Date	Anticipated completion: 2016
Height	214 m and 204 m	140 storeys
GFA	99,400 sqm
Sector	Residential

Gross skygarden/skycourt area	5,992 sqm
Number of skygardens/skycourts	2
% of skygardens/skycourts to built-up area	7.5%

'Three public bridges connect two slender towers at different levels – underground, at the street and in the sky. Catering to the demands and desires of different residents, age groups and cultures, the bridges are landscaped and equipped for a variety of activities traditionally restricted to the ground.'

—Bjarke Ingels

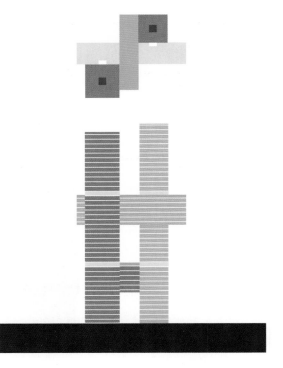

Cross # Towers are a pair of residential structures situated in Seoul's Yongsan international business district and will become a recognisable marker of the new cultural and commercial centre of the city. The design includes two towers with heights of 214 metres and 204 metres. The exceeding building mass is transformed into an upper and lower horizontal bar, which bridge the two towers at 140 metres and 70 metres height. The two towers are additionally connected through the arrival bar at the ground level and a courtyard below ground. Both the upper and lower bridge incorporate skycourts and roof-mounted skygardens that are accessible to residents and permit outdoors activities. Furthermore, the courtyard at the heart of the development is an integral part of the overall architectural design. Residents and visitors are able to enjoy the views towards the neighbouring towers and have visual connectivity from the retail zone across the courtyard. The outer landscape concept aims to combine the charm of traditional courtyard spaces with the modernity of the objects. These towers will accommodate over 600 high-end residences and amenities, including a library, gallery space and kindergarten.*

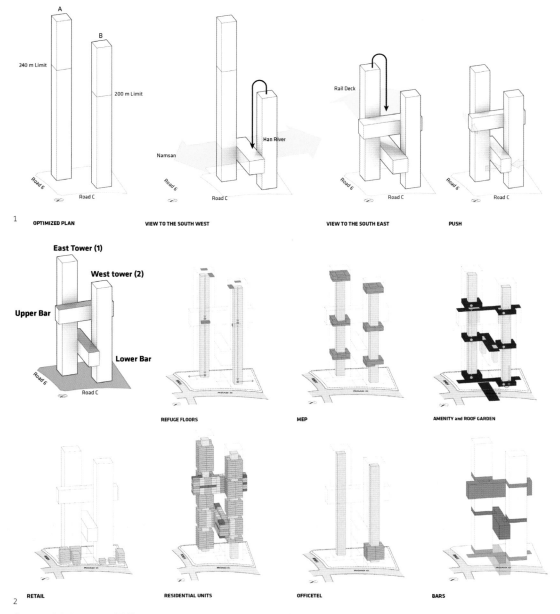

1

OPTIMIZED PLAN

240 m Limit

200 m Limit

A

B

Road 6

Road C

VIEW TO THE SOUTH WEST

Namsan

Han River

Road 6

Road C

VIEW TO THE SOUTH EAST

Rail Deck

Road 6

Road C

PUSH

Road 6

Road C

East Tower (1)

West tower (2)

Upper Bar

Lower Bar

Road 6

Road C

REFUGE FLOORS

MEP

AMENITY and ROOF GARDEN

RETAIL

RESIDENTIAL UNITS

OFFICETEL

BARS

2

1. Conceptual design process © BIG
2. Independent systems within the towers © BIG
* With thanks to BIG for providing part of this text

Rendering of *Cross # Towers*. Seoul © BIG

1. View of main skygarden © BIG
2. Landscaped area on skygarden © BIG
3. Aerial view of overlapping skygardens © BIG

Angkasa Raya

Architect	Büro Ole Scheeren
Location	Kuala Lumpur, Malaysia
Date	Anticipated completion: 2016
Height	268 m | 65 storeys
GFA	165,000 sqm
Sector	Commercial office + residential + hospitality

Gross skygarden/skycourt area	13,780 sqm
Number of skygardens/skycourts	4
% of skygardens/skycourts to built-up area	8.4%

'Angkasa Raya demonstrates possibilities for the amplification of life and activities within the heart of one of Asia's great capitals. Lush green gardens and terraces offer intimacies within the extreme urban density of the surrounding metropolis, while carefully shaded façades and a naturally ventilated atrium underline the environmental responsibility of the design.'

–Büro Ole Scheeren

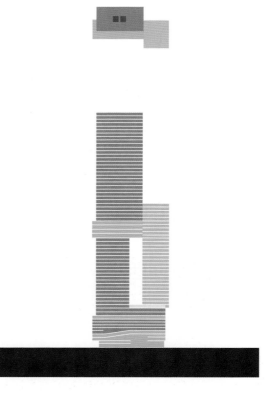

Angkasa Raya is a mixed-use high-rise development located in the heart of Kuala Lumpur city centre, directly opposite the Petronas Twin Towers. The programme includes commercial offices, a luxury hotel, serviced residences, retail and food and beverage space. Between two of the vertical blocks are the 'sky levels', which contain a bar, restaurant, outdoor dining areas, infinity pool edge, banquet hall and other multifunctional leisure and business spaces with views of the Kuala Lumpur skyline amongst the verdant greenery. At 120 metres above the city floor, there are four levels of tropical gardens and metropolitan activity, which will commonly be known as the 'Sky Gardens'. The development's inclusion of urban greenery at the ground and sky levels creates a series of outdoor landscaped activity social spaces that provide numerous areas for flora and vegetation. These areas not only promote environments for social interaction but also help in the reduction of carbon footprint as a result of the insulating properties of green roofs, and the natural shading effect of the horizontal slabs of the ground and sky levels. Furthermore, the tower façades are wrapped with modular aluminium sun-shading devices, geometrically optimised and carefully adjusted to reduce the solar heat gained under the intense sun.*

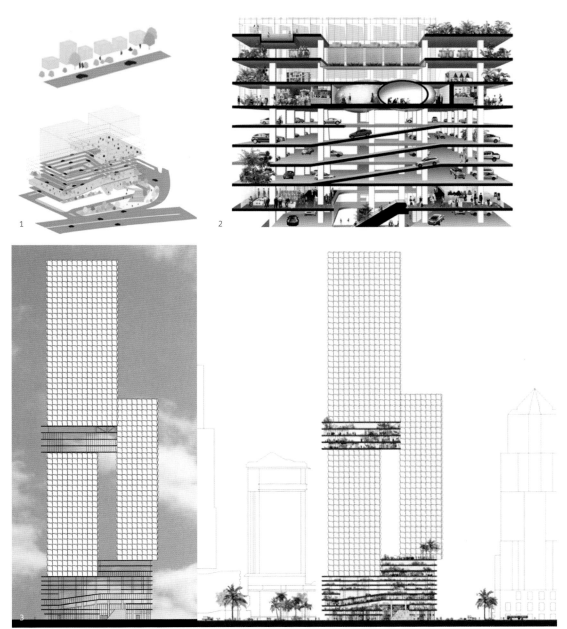

1. Diagram of relationship between skycourt and the street © Büro Ole Scheeren
2. Sectional perspective © Büro Ole Scheeren
3. Building elevation and section © Büro Ole Scheeren
* With thanks to Büro Ole Scheeren for providing part of this text

Rendering of *Angkasa Raya*, Kuala Lumpur © Büro Ole Scheeren

1. View from skycourt © Büro Ole Scheeren
2. Interior planted atrium space © Büro Ole Scheeren
3. Exterior view of skycourt © Büro Ole Scheeren
4. View from street level © Büro Ole Scheeren

Velo Towers

Architect	Asymptote Architecture: Hani Rashid + Lise Anne Couture
Location	Seoul, South Korea
Date	Anticipated completion: confidential
Height	153 m | 40 storeys
GFA	Confidential
Sector	Residential

Gross skygarden/skycourt area	Confidential
Number of skygardens/skycourts	14
% of skygardens/skycourts to built-up area	Confidential

'With a collection of roof gardens, shared amenities and internal circulation around light-filled open atrium spaces, the vertically distributed massing elements create unique six- to eight-storey residential communities on the skyline. The towers are joined by two bridge structures that house shared public amenities, and act as neighbourhood-scale "connectors" for the towers' residents.'

—Asymptote Architecture

The *Velo Towers* are a series of residential structures that collectively incorporate 500 apartments in the Yongsan international business district of Seoul. By breaking down the scale and massing of the two distinct towers into interconnected circular and oblong volumes, the Velo project proposes an alternative architectural and urbanistic response to the repetitive and monolithic austerity of conventional tower design. 'With a collection of roof gardens, shared amenities and internal circulation around light-filled open atrium spaces, the vertically distributed massing elements create unique six- to eight-storey residential communities on the skyline. The towers are joined by two bridge structures that house shared public amenities, and act as neighbourhood-scale "connectors" for the towers' residents.' The building's raised plinth hovers above the communal landscape surrounding the base of the towers while the skybridge floats 30 storeys above, housing fitness and recreation centres, lounges, pools, spas and cafés along with a skygarden providing spectacular views over the entire skygarden Yongsan site.*

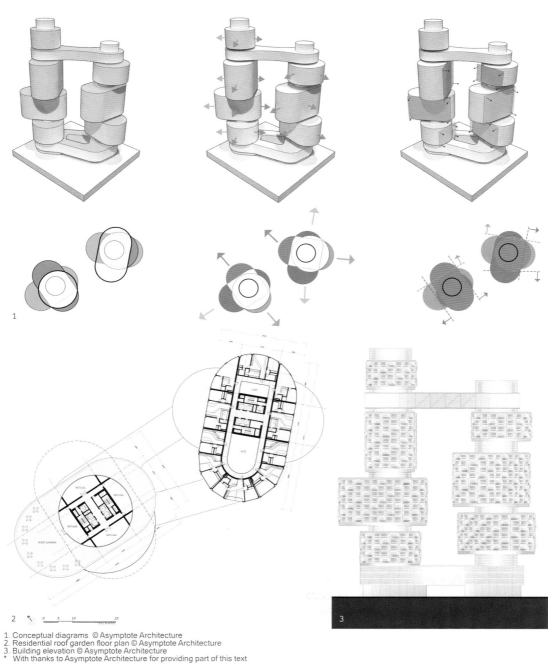

1. Conceptual diagrams © Asymptote Architecture
2. Residential roof garden floor plan © Asymptote Architecture
3. Building elevation © Asymptote Architecture
*   With thanks to Asymptote Architecture for providing part of this text

Rendering of *Velo Towers*, Seoul © Asymptote Architecture

1. Aerial view of skygarden © Asymptote Architecture
2. View of building façade and bridge links © Asymptote Architecture
3. View of exterior plinth © Asymptote Architecture
4. Aerial view of bridge links © Asymptote Architecture

SBF Tower

Architect	Atelier Hollein
Location	Shenzhen, China
Date	Anticipated completion: 2014
Height	200 m	42 storeys
GFA	80,500 sqm
Sector	Commercial office

Gross skygarden/skycourt area	4,320 sqm
Number of skygardens/skycourts	75
% of skygardens/skycourts to built-up area	5.1%

'Each individual floor is seemingly different; deep setbacks and far outreaching cantilevers interchange along the imaginary façade line and are overgrown with plants. These sky garden-levels also have the advantage that their purposely versatile outer appearance is very flexible and can easily answer individual situations.'

—Atelier Hollein

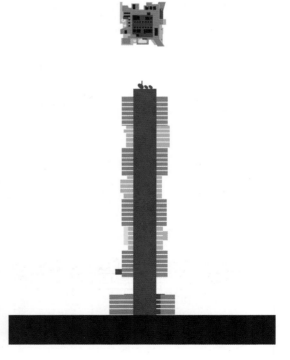

The *SBF Tower* becomes a dominant statement within the high-rise structures of Shenzhen, and occupies an exposed corner position of the cluster. The 42-storey tall building is a simple square of 45 metres by 45 metres, with an overall height of 200 metres, and features a total floor area of 80,500 square metres above ground. A podium partially frames the tower at the base, where the entrance area, public business hall and restaurant are located. The tower rises on top as a sculptured building with vertical gardens and recreational amenities that are integrated into the architecture, giving the tower a very distinctive appearance. Vertically, the tower is a layered structure featuring two different zones of five and six floors, each of which repeatedly alternate three and four times. Each workplace zone has six identical floors with a square outer perimeter. The alternate five-storey zones are highly complex in their outer appearance: Each individual floor is seemingly different; deep setbacks and far-outreaching cantilevers interchange along the imaginary façade line and are overgrown with plants. These skycourt levels also have the advantage that their purposely versatile outer appearance is very flexible and can easily answer individual situations.*

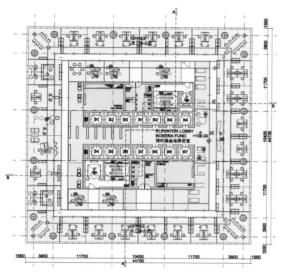

BOXLEVEL 30
標準楼层

1

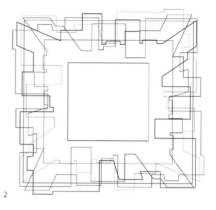

2

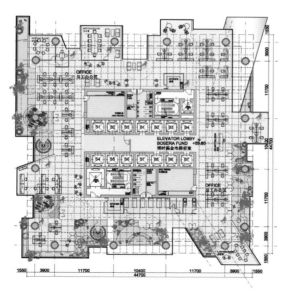

SKYGARDEN FLOOR D 13
花园层D

3

4

1. Box-level floor plan © Courtesy of Atelier Hollein
2. Tower logo © Courtesy of Atelier Hollein
3. Skygarden floor plan © Courtesy of Atelier Hollein
4. Rear elevation © Courtesy of Atelier Hollein
*   With thanks to Atelier Hollein for providing part of this text

Rendering of *SBF Tower*, Shenzhen © Atelier Hollein

1. Detailed view of exterior © Atelier Hollein
2. View of skyline © Atelier Hollein

Sky Village, Living in the Cloud

Architect	MVRDV
Location	Seoul, South Korea
Date	Anticipated completion: 2016
Height	260 m | 54 storeys
GFA	128,000 sqm
Sector	Residential + commercial office

Gross skygarden/skycourt area	14,357 sqm
Number of skygardens/skycourts	22
% of skygardens/skycourts to built-up area	11.2%

'By integrating public programme to the cloud the typology adds in a more social way to the city. Inside the cloud, besides the residential function, 14,357 m² of amenities are located: the sky lounge – a large connecting atrium, a wellness centre, conference centre, fitness studio, various pools, restaurants and cafés. On top of the cloud are a series of public and private outside spaces, patios, decks, gardens and pools.'

—MVRDV

The Cloud is a luxury twin-tower mixed-use residential development in the Yongsan international business district of Seoul. The development contains 9,000 square metres of officetel (office-hotel) and 25,000 square metres panoramic apartments with specific layouts. The top floors of both towers are reserved for penthouse apartments of 1,200 square metres with private roof gardens. The two residential towers are punctuated by the inclusion of a multi-layered recreational environment that alludes to the form of a cloud. The cloud will sit at the 27th floor of the building structure and seeks to place facilities often associated with the ground into the sky – thus freeing up the ground plane to allow landscape architect Martha Schwartz to design several gardens, pools and plazas to surround the towers. Its pixellated form will spread along 10 floors and will accommodate a connecting atrium, a wellness centre, restaurants, cafés, gym facilities and a conference centre. On top of the cloud are a series of public and private outside spaces, patios, decks, gardens and pools. To allow fast access the cloud is accessible by special express elevators. On the ground floor, townhouses will be built, while the higher floors provide space for luxury apartments. The top floors will be reserved for penthouses with private skygardens. *

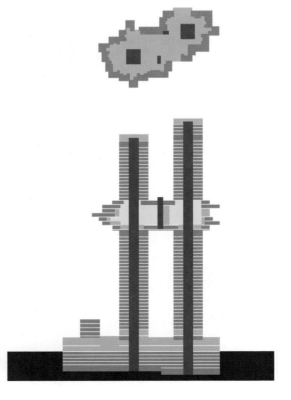

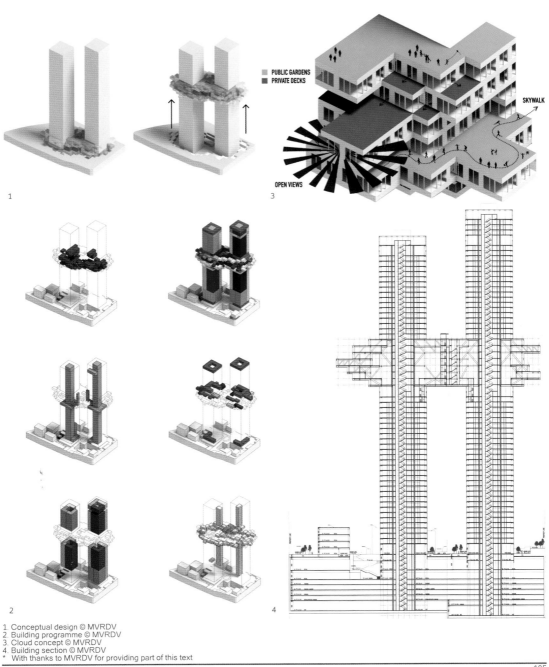

PUBLIC GARDENS
PRIVATE DECKS

SKYWALK

OPEN VIEWS

1

3

2

4

1. Conceptual design © MVRDV
2. Building programme © MVRDV
3. Cloud concept © MVRDV
4. Building section © MVRDV
* With thanks to MVRDV for providing part of this text

Rendering of *The Cloud*, Seoul © MVRDV

1. Bird's eye view of cloud podium © MVRDV
2. Skygarden decks © MVRDV
3. Lobby within *The Cloud* © MVRDV
4. Exterior space on *The Cloud* © MVRDV

Dancing Dragons

Architect	Adrian Smith + Gordon Gill
Location	Seoul, South Korea
Date	Anticipated completion: TBD
Height	450 m and 390 m | 88 and 77 storeys
GFA	123,093 sqm and 111,951 sqm
Sector	Residential + commercial office + retail

Gross skygarden/skycourt area	510/388 sqm
Number of skygardens/skycourts	2
% of skygardens/skycourts to built-up area	0.41%/0.35%

'Dancing Dragons' scale-like skin is also a performative element. Gaps between its overlapping panels feature operable 600 mm vents through which air can circulate, making the skin "breathable" like that of certain animals.'
　　　　　　　　　　　　　　　　　–Adrian Smith + Gordon Gill

Dancing Dragons is a mixed-use development in the Yongsan international business district of Seoul. It will include residential, officetel and retail elements and consists of slender, sharply angled mini-towers cantilevered around a central core. The design aesthetic is highly contemporary yet informed by aspects of traditional Korean culture. The mini-towers feature a dramatic series of diagonal massing cuts that create living spaces that float beyond the structure. This recalls the eaves of traditional Korean pagodas – a design theme echoed both in the geometry of the building skin and the jutting canopies at the towers' base. The theme is extended in the building skin, which suggests the scales of fish and Korean mythical creatures such as dragons, which seem to dance around the core – hence the project's name. (Yongsan, the name of the overall development, means 'Dragon Hill' in Korean.) The mini-tower cuts offer the opportunity for special high-value penthouse duplex units with spectacular 360-degree views of downtown Seoul and the adjacent Han River, along with an abundance of natural light. Recreational activites found within its skycourts include a wine-tasting room, spa, lounge, games room, theatre, driving range, gymnasium and fitness suites.*

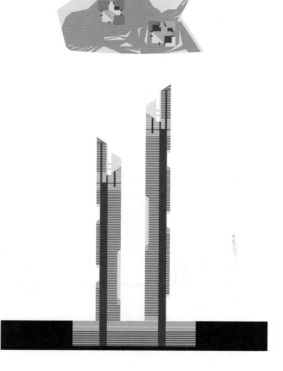

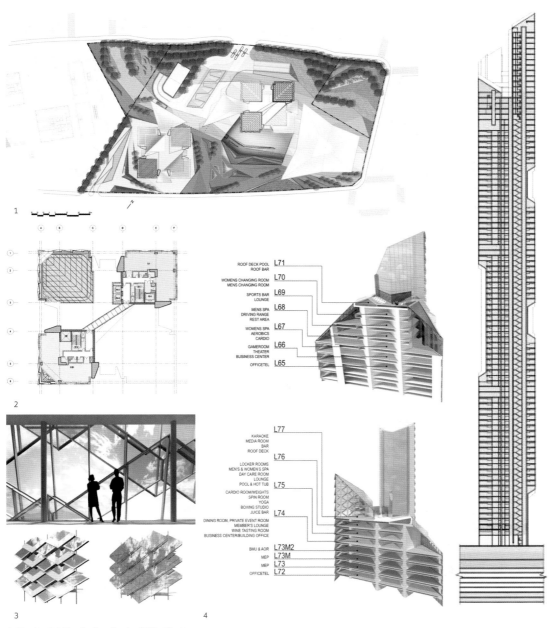

1

2

3   4

1. Site plan © Adrian Smith + Gordon Gill Architecture
2. Roof plan © Adrian Smith + Gordon Gill Architecture
3. Skin diagrams © Adrian Smith + Gordon Gill Architecture
4. Amenities and building sections © Adrian Smith + Gordon Gill Architecture
* With thanks to Adrian Smith + Gordon Gill Architecture for providing part of this text

Rendering of the *Dancing Dragons*. Seoul © Adrian Smith + Gordon Gill Architecture

1. Internal view of atrium © Adrian Smith + Gordon Gill Architecture
2. View from staircase © Adrian Smith + Gordon Gill Architecture
3. Rooftop event space © Adrian Smith + Gordon Gill Architecture
4. Main entrance © Adrian Smith + Gordon Gill Architecture

The Veil

Architect	Pomeroy Studio
Location	Kuala Lumpur, Malaysia
Date	Anticipated completion: 2015
Height	150 m	38 storeys
GFA	51,500 sqm
Sector	Residential + commercial office + hotel

Gross skygarden/skycourt area	1,921 sqm
Number of skygardens/skycourts	4
% of skygardens/skycourts to built-up area	3.7%

'The Veil presents a paradigm shift away from the single-use tower to embrace a mix of uses that redefines the 21st century tall building within Kuala Lumpur's city centre. The use programme comprises office, retail, food and beverage, hotel and penthouses that are separated by skycourts – effectively providing a vertical extrusion of the city.'

–Pomeroy Studio

The Veil is a 40-storey mixed-use tall building in the heart of Kuala Lumpur city centre. Generous naturally lit office floor plates have been designed to British Council of Offices standards, and are separated by skycourts that contain the hotel lobby and public amenity spaces. The hotel's position above the office provides an opportunity to glean the predominant views of the KL Tower and Petronas Twin Towers. Penthouse suites and a sky restaurant crown the development, each with their own skycourts that furthermore provide a lifestyle entertainment and recreational space for their occupants. The green agenda is actively pursued in the environmental design of the tall building, whilst ensuring that the economic sustainability of the project is not compromised given its conformity to international design and planning standards for the office, hotel and residential components. The 'veil' acts as an environmental screen in response to the low-angle sun to the east and the west, and helps reduce direct solar heat gain. It is further enhanced by the incorporation of vertical greenery that in the same instance embraces the cultural sensitivities of the region – namely in the form of a geometric patterned screen. This references the traditional screens, called *mashrabiya*, which permit daylight whilst providing shade.

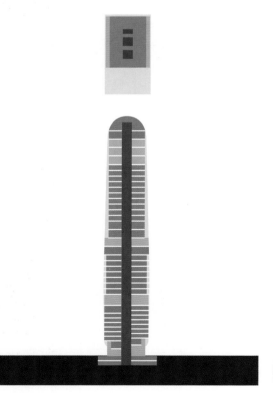

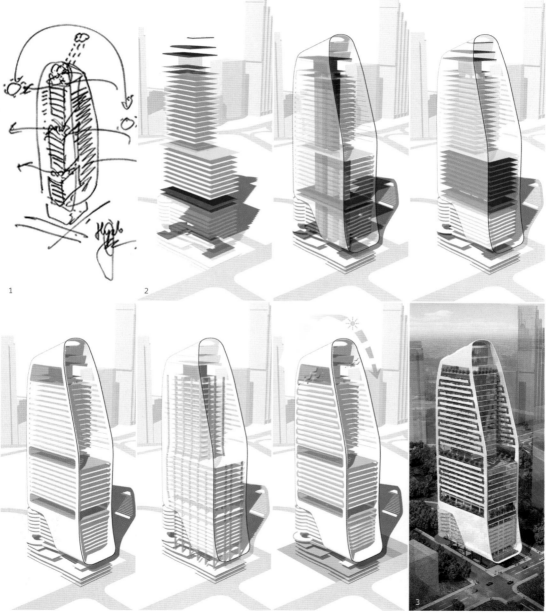

1. Conceptual sketch © Pomeroy Studio
2. Concept principle study diagrams © Pomeroy Studio
3. Aerial rendering © Pomeroy Studio

Rendering of *The Veil*, Kuala Lumpur © Pomeroy Studio

1. Street-level view © Pomeroy Studio
2. View of building in context © Pomeroy Studio
3. View of skygarden © Pomeroy Studio

Columbia University Medical Center

Architect   Diller Scofidio + Renfro
                Gensler (Executive Architect)
Location   New York City, United States
Date   Anticipated completion: 2016
Height   N/A | 14 storeys
GFA   9,290 sqm
Sector   Civic and institutional

Gross skygarden/skycourt area	Confidential
Number of skygardens/skycourts	2
% of skygardens/skycourts to built-up area	2.9%

'The "Study Cascade" is the principle design strategy of the building – a network of social and study spaces distributed across oversize landings along an intricate 14-storey stair. The Study Cascade creates a single interconnected space the height of the building, stretching from the ground-floor lobby to the top, and conducive to collaborative, team-based learning and teaching.'

–Diller Scofidio + Renfro

The *Columbia University Medical Center (CUMC)* is situated in the heart of the city of New York. The 14-storey building will provide space and facilities for physicians, surgeons, nurses, dentists and doctors in training, and is intended to present a transparent, healthy learning and working environment that includes vertical spaces for socialising and relaxation. It will accommodate rooms for study and places to recreate real-life medical situations in simulation rooms. Surrounded with green areas, the new campus addition will revitalise outdoor spaces while the form's glass-enclosed vertical stack of social and public areas will form a notable landmark to the skyline of Manhattan. 'The "Study Cascade" is the principle design strategy of the building – a network of social and study spaces distributed across oversize landings along an intricate 14-storey stair. The Study Cascade creates a single interconnected space the height of the building, stretching from the ground-floor lobby to the top, and conducive to collaborative, team-based learning and teaching.' The Study Cascade interiors are complemented by a network of south-facing outdoor rooms and skycourts that are clad with cement panels and wood. Additional rooms will support the university's newly integrated curriculum of team-based learning.*

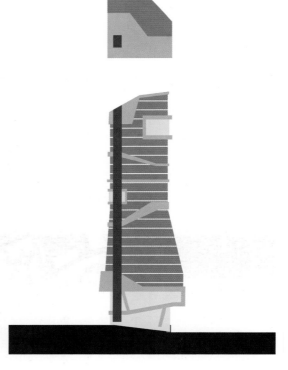

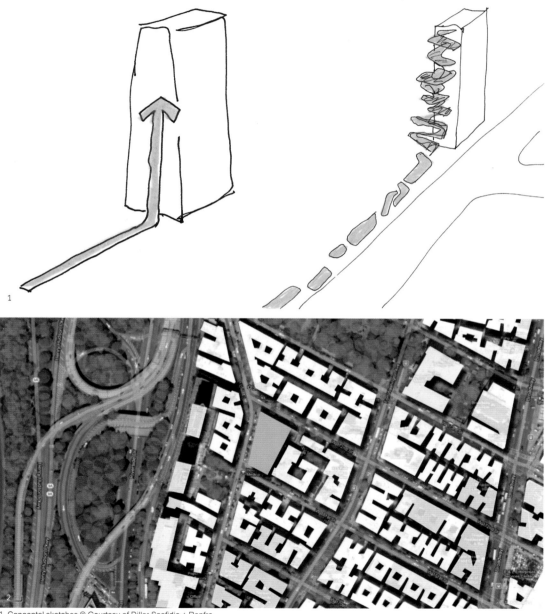

1. Conceptal sketches © Courtesy of Diller Scofidio + Renfro
2. Project location
*   With thanks to Diller Scofidio + Renfro for providing part of this text

Rendering of *Columbia University Medical Center*, New York © Courtesy of Diller Scofidio + Renfro

1. Auditorium entrance © Courtesy of Diller Scofidio + Renfro
2. Café interior © Courtesy of Diller Scofidio + Renfro
3. Exterior view of elevated café © Courtesy of Diller Scofidio + Renfro
4. Floating terrace landcape design © Courtesy of Diller Scofidio + Renfro

3.4 Future vision

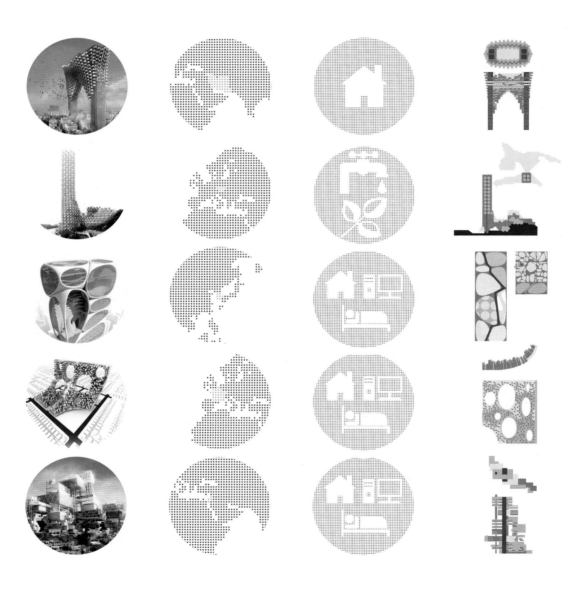

Tehran Tower

Design   Mahdi Kamboozia
              Alireza Esfandiari
              Nima Daehghani
              Mohammad Ashkbar Sefat
Location Tehran, Iran
Sector   Residential

'Tehran is the capital of Iran and the Tehran Province. WIth an estimated population of 8,429,807, it is also Iran's largest urban area and city. Tehran suffers from severe air pollution and the city is often covered by smog, making breathing difficult and causing widespread pulmonary illnesses. It is estimated that about 27 people die each day from pollution-related diseases, and it causes more than $1 billion in damage to the city. The high density and poor living conditions are due to the axial growth originally masterplanned, which no longer accommodates the unplanned growth of the city. Our main idea in this project is to increase the vertical density and decrease the horizontal density by developing green lands and retaining the most important buildings of the site. Our method is to build the parking first to service the city, remove the old buildings and then replace them with new ones in the proposed tower. This allows the maintenance of the functioning existing buildings, while the poorly functioning buildings will be replaced by the proposed Tehran Tower. This tower will supply 1,200 residential units, and occupy only 1,200 square metres of ground area due to its minimal footprint.'

Mahdi Kamboozia
Alireza Esfandiari
Nima Dehghani
Mohammad Ashkbar Sefat

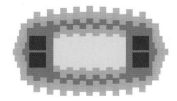

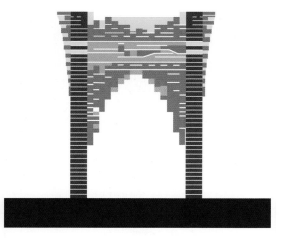

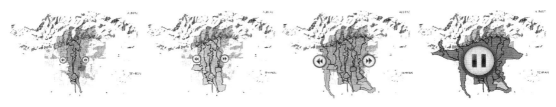

Tehran growth is oriental-occidental.It doesn't match with its geographical realities.

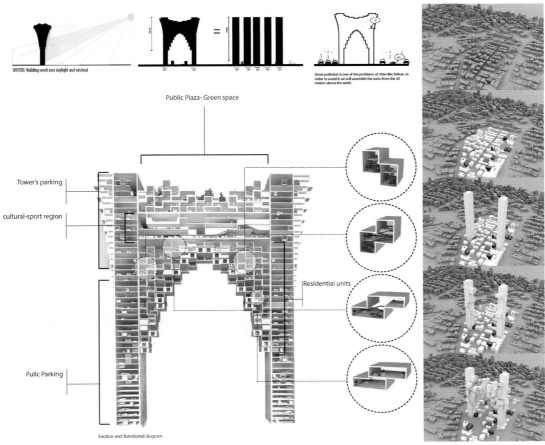

WINTER/ Building needs mor daylight and sun heat

Noise pollution is one of the problems of cities like Tehran .In order to avoid it we will assemble the units from the 50 meters above the earth.

Public Plaza- Green space

Tower's parking

cultural-sport region

Residential units

Pulic Parking

Section and functional diagram

© Courtesy of eVolo

© Courtesy of eVolo

© Courtesy of eVolo

Skyscraper Garden

Design   Michaela Dejdarova
                Michal Votruba
Location   Prague, Czech Republic
Sector   Infrastructure/vertical farming

'Vertical farms seem to be one of the best solutions for encouraging agriculture in the cities. They are a smart solution where transportation costs and pollutants are reduced. This proposal conceived by Michaela Dejdarova and Michal Votruba is located on the outskirts of Prague, Czech Republic and it is intended to be a communal farm for the city. The structure consists of clusters of tetrahedrons grouped to create an exoskeleton that peels from the ground and supports hundreds of green terraces for agriculture. The novelty of the idea is that it could be developed in stages because of the modularity of all the components. It could grow and spread according to demand and could also be easily dismantled and transported to other locations. As with other vertical farms, this project uses rainwater collection systems and solar panels as its main source of water and energy.'

Michaela Dejdarova
Michal Votruba

© Courtesy of eVolo

26-HEDRON

TETRAHEDRON

CUBE

© Courtesy of eVolo

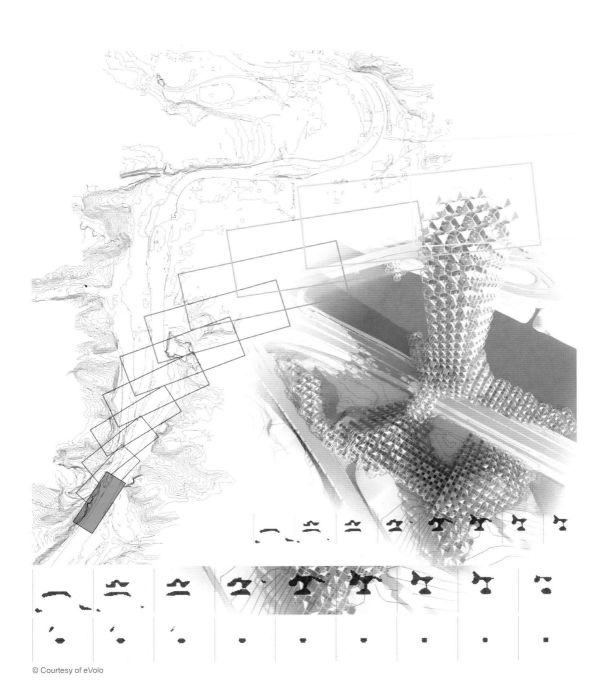

© Courtesy of eVolo

CollageScape

Design Kang Woo-Young
Location Incheon, South Korea
Sector Mixed use

'In the modern city, a natural landscape no longer exists, and only an artificial environment is extended through the horizontal and repetitive construction. The goal of the project is to recover the lack of nature within the tedious mechanical urban image, by using a metaphorical landscape reproduction process. The architecture has evolved in the city as skyscrapers that are monuments that symbolize the city's identity. This is common to the contemporary city, though there are many skyscrapers that have been abandoned. Terrain is not a flat plate but a contour-based surface. From this point of view, a curve is the natural line of our physical world, and curved surfaces represent the typical form of landscape. As the architecture is a logically integrated system with art and technology, it is similar to formal mathematical systems that study the relation between elements, with the purpose of enriching existing structures or creating new ones. For this reason, isosurface, a logic-based mathematical surface, is adopted to represent the logical form of terrain. The main programme in this project is a vertical park which contains outdoor recreation activities, walking, jogging, and climbing. The whole building consists of partial buildings with a form of block, each individual block having its own programme and connection to each other.'

Kang Woo-Young

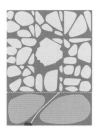

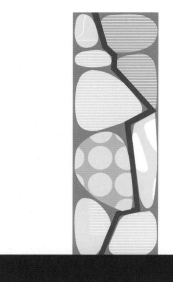

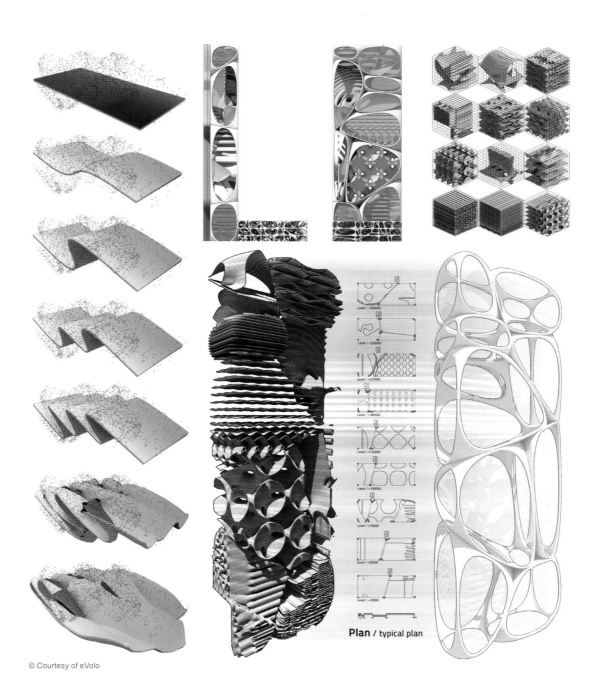

Plan / typical plan

© Courtesy of eVolo

© Courtesy of eVolo

© Courtesy of eVolo

Folded City

Design Adrien Piebourg
      Bastien Papetti
Location Global application
Sector Mixed use

'How can we live vertically? Climbing higher and higher does not seem to change the way we live. Most people wish to live in individual houses, so we have to be interested in the pavilion. But the problem is now well established: sprawl, lack of diversity and density, and poverty of an architectural uniformity, among other problems. Our question is: how can we encourage everyone to live at home with the qualities desired within the heart of the city? The function of living would be challenged in the object. The house becomes as smart as the Smartphone, and incorporates multiple applications. One application per floor. The elevator is for the house what the Internet is for the phone. A necessary parameter! Now you can "zap" your life spatially. Imagine yourself in your room, put on your slippers, go in your elevator, and zap! You will be almost instantaneously in your living room, your garage, your favourite bar or business place, or the park where you go jogging!'

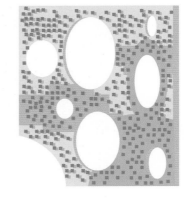

Adrien Piebourg
Bastien Papetti

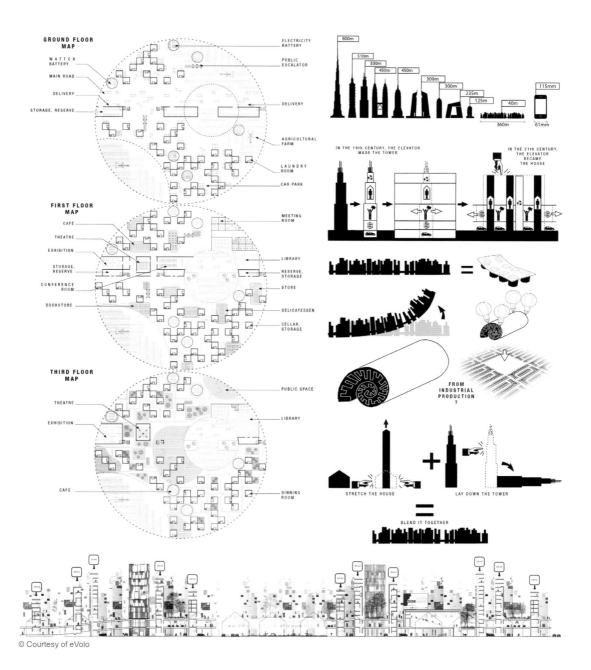

© Courtesy of eVolo

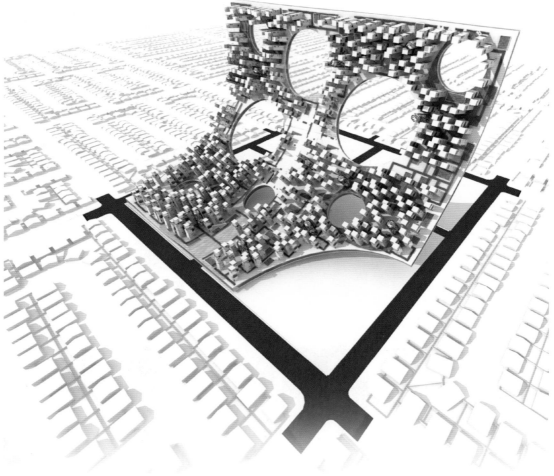

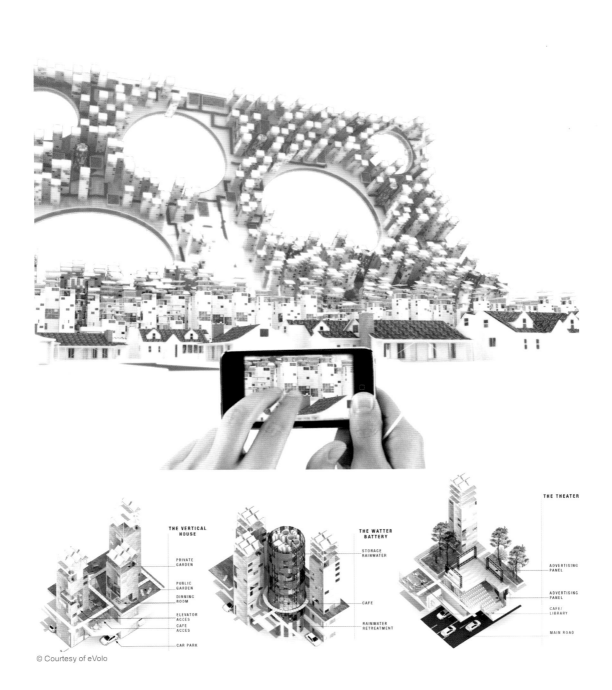

THE VERTICAL HOUSE
- PRIVATE GARDEN
- PUBLIC GARDEN
- DINNING ROOM
- ELEVATOR ACCES
- CAFE ACCES
- CAR PARK

THE WATTER BATTERY
- STORAGE RAINWATER
- CAFE
- RAINWATER RETREATMENT

THE THEATER
- ADVERTISING PANEL
- ADVERTISING PANEL
- CAFE/ LIBRARY
- MAIN ROAD

© Courtesy of eVolo

District 3 – Skyscraper of Liberation

Design   Xiaoliang Lu
               Yikai Lin
Location Border of Palestine and Israel
Sector   Mixed use

'On the borders of two regions at war, those who suffer the greatest are the citizens who simply want peace for their nation. Often, warring regions build great walls between them. But do such walls truly solve conflict? They don't, say the designers of the *District 3 – Skyscraper of Liberation* project. Instead, walls obstruct mutual understanding and intensify the discrepancy. This project considers the border of Israel and Palestine, which is defined by three districts: an Israeli district, a Palestinian district and a third, which is a zone where the borders are separated by a wall. This wall will be removed and replaced with a skyscraper, transforming the isolated and hate-filled area with one that is shared and fosters reconciliation. The skyscraper can only be entered by Palestinians and Israelis who are non-violent and seek peace and cooperation, and is administered by the United Nations. The skyscraper will have many programmes inside to foster cultural and social exchanges between the two countries. These programmes include a farmer's market, a soccer stadium, a museum, a school, performing arts and assembly spaces, a zoo, a hotel, shopping and business spaces, and farmland at the very top. Residential complexes are connected to the skyscraper peripherally.'

Xiaoliang Lu
Yikai Lin

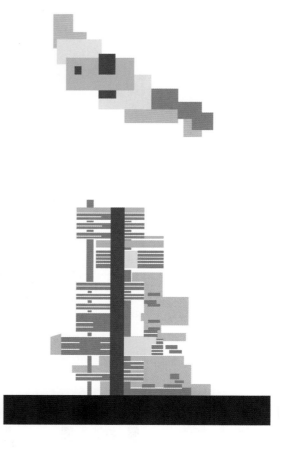

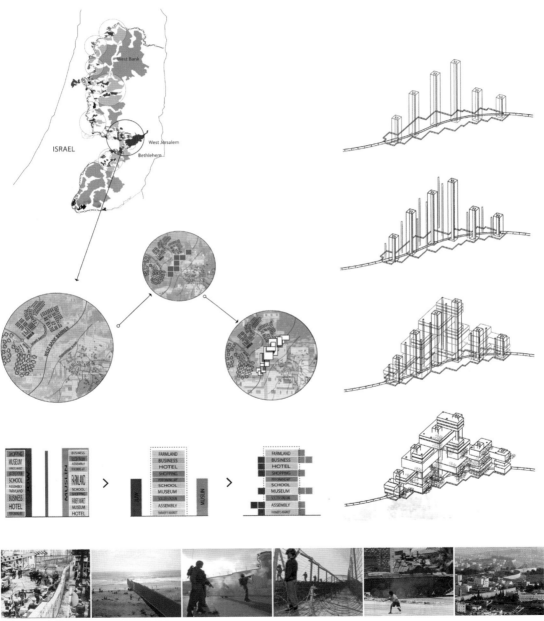

© Courtesy of eVolo

© Courtesy of eVolo

© Courtesy of eVolo

Borough No. 6

Design   John Houser
Location   New York City, United States
Sector   Mixed use

'The unprecedented population growth of mega-cites around the world requires the sustained increase of urban density. Over the past century the pressure from population growth was relieved with the vertical expansion of the city. To fulfill the population demands of tomorrow, growth in building density will be forced to expand in all axes. Situated above the existing urban fabric, this building occupies the space between 22nd and 14th Street and 6th and 7th Avenue in New York City. The size of the structure creates interdependency, and allows for the formation of new communities within the already-dense housing grid. Woven into the residential fabric of the grid, large office towers provide a workplace for the residents of the structure. These towers unfold to allow for a large public park cut high above the city, maintaining the necessary public access to nature. Far removed from the intensity of urban life, the park provides residents and visitors an escape to nature while still maintaining a unique visual link with the city. The building is interconnected with a massive expansion of the current New York subway system. Trains within the structure move in all directions, servicing stations at all levels. Stations are embedded within the grid structure and linked to pedestrian bridges which act as the main arteries of transportation. The collection of these parts reaches a critical mass, allowing the structure to exist as an autonomous entity within the city, a new radical prototype for a 6th borough.'

John Houser

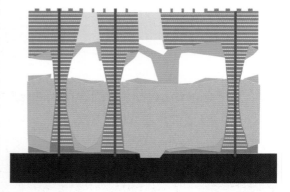

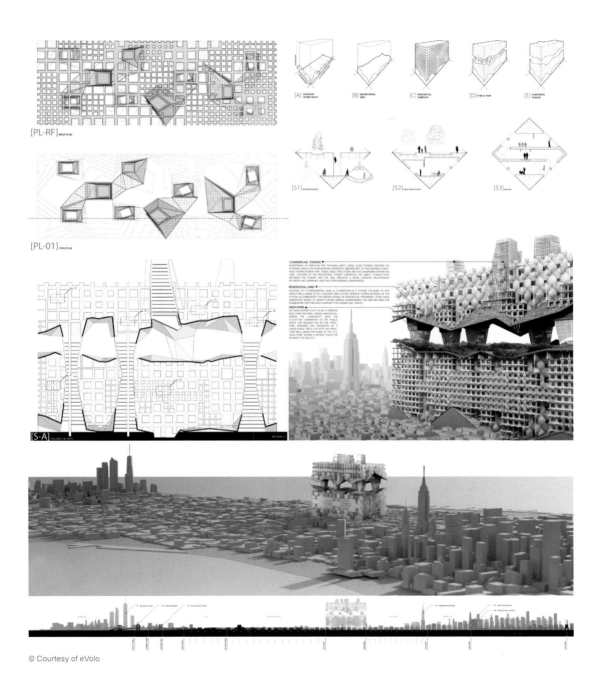

© Courtesy of eVolo

© Courtesy of eVolo

© Courtesy of eVolo

3D Green: Vertical Farmland Inserted in an Existing Urban Fabric

Design   Yiqing Jiang
                Ying Tao
Location   Shanghai, China
Sector   Vertical park and farm

'This project examines the idea of developing a vertical park and farm between skyscrapers in Shanghai, China. Over the last 20 years Shanghai has grown exponentially due to the massive migration from rural to urban China. This has led to the development of hundreds of skyscrapers that today define the city's skyline. Unfortunately, the number of public parks and recreational areas has not increased and the city is now a large block of concrete and glass. This project uses the structure of three contiguous skyscrapers to attach a vertical park that will serve as prototype for the city. The new park would provide a recreational green space to the office towers and a new lung to the city. In addition, the park is equipped with wind turbines and photovoltaic cells for wind and solar energy harvesting.'

Yiqing Jiang
Ying Tao

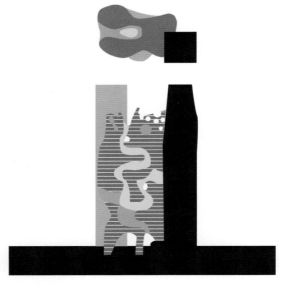

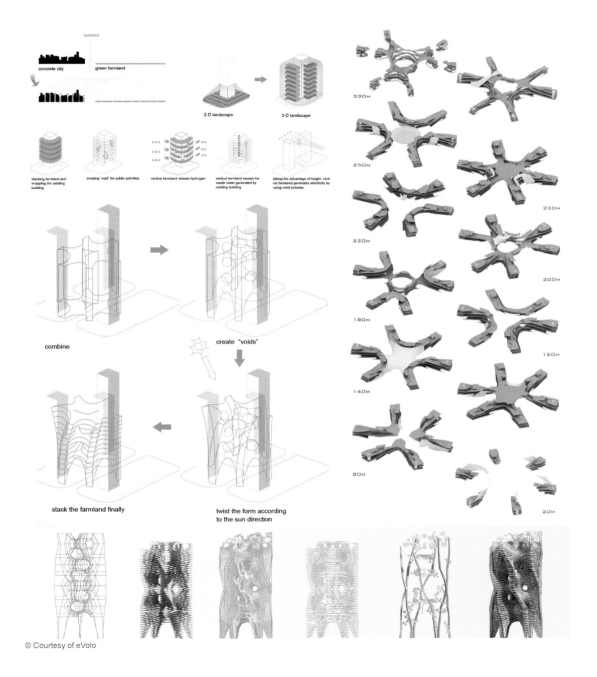

isolated

concrete city   green farmland

2-D landscape   3-D landscape

stacking farmland and   creating "void" for public activities   vertical farmland release hydrogen   vertical farmland reuses the   taking the advantage of height, verti-
wrapping the existing   waste water generated by   cal farmland generates electricity by
building   existing building   using wind turbines.

combine   create "voids"

stack the farmland finally   twist the form according
                                   to the sun direction

330M

250M

230M

220M

200M

180M

160M

140M

80M

20M

© Courtesy of eVolo

© Courtesy of eVolo

© Courtesy of eVolo

Elevated Connectivity

Design	Adam Nakagoshi
	Thao Nguyen
Location	Global application
Sector	Infrastructure

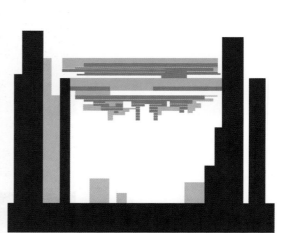

'Towers are architectural monuments elevating the city dweller from the active urban ground plane. At the height of the tower, one's experience becomes isolated from the public domain and the urban condition becomes physically and experientially cropped from one's awareness. The proposal seeks to reroute the spatially and experientially isolated occurrences at the towers' height and tie these loose ends together to allow for space to move fluidly and continuously and thus reuniting the inhabitant with the core experience. Furthermore, the proposal will provide a means to reactivate and energize the spaces that have become inactive or abandoned and thus interjecting them with more universally accessible and sustainable functions. The proposal is shaped within three phases of architectural, spatial, and urban intervention. These phases collectively will provide an elevated layer of modern communication that will redefine and introduce the city back into the frames of the experiencing self. The architectural phase of the proposal will bridge the elevated points of isolation through a horizontal tower to seal the voids above the city grid. These various points of connection will allow for an architectural fabric that is populated with public and private functions. The lost communication of cities is now given an opportunity to materialize; physically and architecturally expressing the connection of people and place.'

Adam Nakagoshi
Thao Nguyen

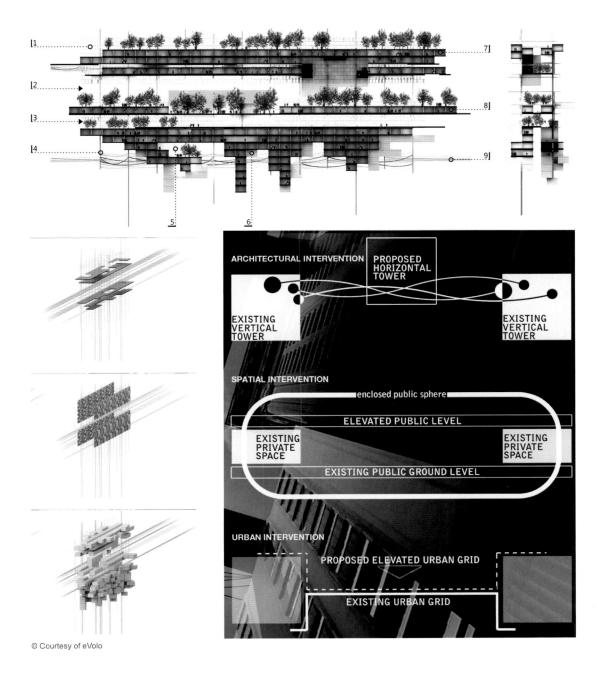

© Courtesy of eVolo

© Courtesy of eVolo

© Courtesy of eVolo

Water Purification Skyscraper

Design	Rezza Rahdian
	Erwin Setiawan
	Ayu Diah Shanti
	Leonardus Chrisnantyo
Location	Jakarta, Indonesia
Sector	Infrastructure

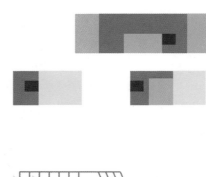

'The city of Jakarta, Indonesia, was originally designed at the confluence of thirteen rivers which were used for transportation and agriculture. The largest of its rivers is the Ciliwung River, which has become extremely polluted during the last couple of decades and is characterized by hundreds of slums inhabited by thousands of people in marginal conditions. The Ciliwung Recovery Programme (CRP) is a project that aims to collect the garbage from the riverbank and purify its water through an ingenious system of mega-filters that operate in three different phases. The first one separates the different types of garbage and utilizes the organic waste to fertilize its soil. The second phase purifies the water by removing dangerous chemicals and adding important minerals to it. The clean water is then fed to the river and to the nearby agricultural fields through a system of capillary tubes. Finally in the third phase all the recyclable waste is processed. One of the most important aspects of this proposal is the elimination of the slums along the river. The majority of the people will live and work at the CRP which could be understood as a new city within Jakarta. The CRP project will be a 100 percent sustainable building that will produce energy through wind, solar, and hydroelectric systems.'

Rezza Rahdian
Erwin Setiawan
Ayu Diah Shanti
Leonardus Chrisnantyo

© Courtesy of eVolo

© Courtesy of eVolo

© Courtesy of eVolo

Urban Nebulizer

Design	Han Jaekyu
	Park Sang Mi
	Kim Ji Hyun
	Park Woo Young
	Lee Kyoung Ho
Location	Daegu, South Korea
Sector	Infrastructure

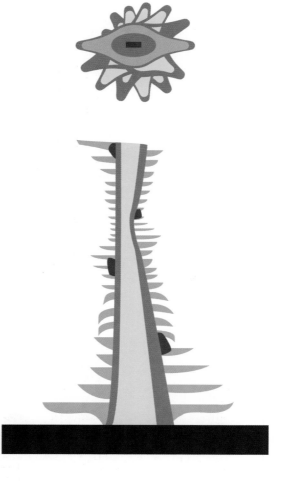

'The site of our plan is located in Daegu and is surrounded by mountains. It is a nationally recognized area due to its landscape and basin. Because of this location, Daegu has a temperature-inversion every quarter of the year. Moreover, industrialization, urbanization and the high density of the city decreased the green zone as well as contaminated the air of an industrial area at the center of the city. This has seriously threatened the health of city dwellers, who are already subjected to severe heat islanding and a high-density environment. The center of a smokestack is designed with a spiral shape much like a tornado to channel air into the upper direction. The spiral tightens as the height increases, to push air out through the top of the structure. Much like the make-up of a pine cone, the windowpane structure is laid one upon another, to create an environment that circulates air and promotes ease of photosynthesis for the plants within the structure. The Urban Nebulizer's dimensions are based on the different factors of each environmental and physical situation. The Urban Nebulizer is supported through a two-part division. One structural element occurs as a massive column in the center of the structure. This column tapers outward closer to the ground, for increased stability. The elevator core is twisted along with the exterior of the structure, allowing for a maintenance of form.'

Han Jaekyu
Park Sang Mi
Kim Ji Hyun
Park Woo Young
Lee Kyoung Ho

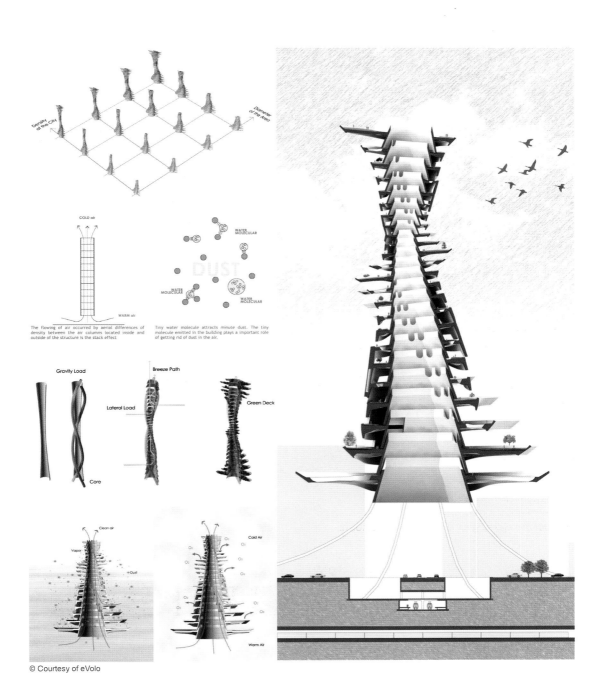

The flowing of air occurred by aerial differences of density between the air columns located inside and outside of the structure is the stack effect

Tiny water molecule attracts minute dust. The tiny molecule emitted in the building plays a important role of getting rid of dust in the air.

COLD air

WARM air

WATER MOLECULAR

DUST

WATER MOLECULAR

WATER MOLECULAR

Density of the City

Diameter of the Area

Gravity Load

Breeze Path

Lateral Load

Green Deck

Core

Clean air

Vapor

Dust

Cold Air

Warm Air

O_2

© Courtesy of eVolo

© Courtesy of eVolo

© Courtesy of eVolo

Towards a vertical urban theory

4. Towards a vertical urban theory

4.1 The skycourt and skygarden: evolutionary observations

We have seen how the quest to replicate the street and the square as a means of freely 'transferring' material goods, knowledge, secrets, movement, culture, spiritual or political message through the semi-public realm has not always provided the full benefit of the freedoms associated with the public domain. The dominant powers vested in the private interests of property developments have often defined how, and when, such social spaces are to be used in order to maintain social control and, from a real estate perspective, preserve asset value. Today, technology further reduces the need for co-presence in space, as society can glean the very same commodities of transference virtually via the internet. This effectively renders the role of public, and even semi-public, space increasingly obsolete. Our sense of being social in public therefore becomes deliberate and planned, as opposed to being the result of daily casual interaction that is spontaneous and unplanned. We pass through an increasing number of privatised transitional social spaces that permit movement in order to visit the retail mall, the cinema, the café or the museum that act as privatised destinations that society plans to meet in.

Skycourts and skygardens have become another social space within the architectural vocabulary of the urban habitat, and currently remains predominantly managed by the corporation or landowner that controls them. They are differentiated by the fundamental truth that they can never be truly public unless they become ceded to state ownership and permit the individual, group or association the freedoms of speech, action and movement that one normally finds in the public domain of the street and the square. The skycourts and skygardens that we have seen similarly demonstrate this. These semi-public realms are, as the academic and architect John Worthington describes, 'seismic creations' – created in an instant, highly classified to their correlating building function, socially controlled by the dominant (private) power and spatially constrained by the structure that retains them. To this end, they have not necessarily promoted a social spontaneity, and their immediate creation is arguably the antithesis to the public realm that incrementally evolves with time and is the result of a continuous contestation of its space by its users. This, in itself, creates interest through the unplanned and unpredictable. Despite the reasons why they are currently not public spaces, we have started to see their evolution given changing social, spatial, environmental, cultural, economic and technological needs that permit the nurturing of public domain characteristics. This may bode well for society's co-presence and may enhance urban life quality as well as the natural and built environment.

We can see in the earlier completed examples that skycourts and skygardens were little more than private terraces; very occasionally planted, and often accessed from the occupied internal areas of the building that retained them. They were often imprinted with the function and control of the dominant power that occupied the habitable space within. Their privatised nature often reduced chances for spontaneity, and the occupants within generally imprinted an implicit control on the skycourt's social use through their observation of such spaces by others. Their control therefore permitted only the occasional use by the worker or resident, which was often dependent on the familiarity of others within its proximity. Their use was predominantly one of the occasional lunchtime visit, or coffee break, and did not necessarily sustain regular patterns of use or heightened social interaction amongst groups (Figure 60).

Figure 60: *Menara Mesiniaga*, Kuala Lumpur: the skycourt as an extension of the internal office function that is used for the occasional informal meeting

However, examples completed more recently show the promise of more 'public'-orientated environments, and their greater usage as an environment for transition, as well as social interaction. Unlike their mono-functional predecessors that were less integrated with circulatory patterns, newer skycourts and skygardens form both internal and external spaces that have become more integrated into the cores of tall buildings. They spatially link vertical methods of circulation and facilitate transition, and socially link occupants through the heightened probability of chance meetings and opportunities for spontaneity. As tall buildings continue to soar higher and embrace an increasingly mixed-use programme, the skycourt has adapted to cater for a greater multiplicity of function. The skycourt, as an interstitial space within the mixed-use tall building, has started to become a 'spatial gel' that glues together the disparate series of land use components as well as beyond, via the skybridge (Figure 61). This has fostered greater usage and a sense of community amongst people from different backgrounds, groups and associations, from different parts of the development and city. With society's heightened

Figure 61: *Biopolis*, Singapore: the skybridge as an opportunity to enhance chance meetings through transitional spaces at multiple levels.

environmental awareness, the incorporation of greenery within skycourts and skygardens has also become more prevalent in the acknowledgement of their environmental, ecological and socio-physiological benefits.

In line with such social, spatial and environmental development, the examples under construction have been the product of an era when alternative social spaces have started to be placed into a hierarchy of urban spaces in terms of scale, use and classification that support existing public spaces, and arguably start to blur boundaries between what is public, semi-public and private. What were once slender viewing balconies have become skycourts and terraces for individuals, families and groups to enjoy as individual private spaces with a greater multiplicity of function (Figure 62). Larger, more neutral skycourts, positioned in prominent and easily accessible parts of the buildings, have started to serve as broader circulatory interchanges that allow the casual interaction on an almost vertical neighbourhood level. When coupled with skybridges, they have become nodes of activity that further heighten social interaction by the presence of both income generating and recreational opportunities. In some countries such as Singapore, the progressive development of skycourts and skygardens has been enabled through economically incentivised legislation in the interests of promoting the cultural identity of a 'greener' city. Such legislative power, with the promise of enhanced permissible developable areas and therefore enhanced return on investment, has allowed such skyrise social spaces to become an increasingly popular addition to the urban architectural vocabulary of the urban habitat.

Banham's comment that 'no architect who considers himself worthy of his craft can bear to stand by and see his design destroyed, especially grand designs in the scale of the city' (Banham, 1976) is having to be re-evaluated given a rapid urbanisation to cater for 70% of the global population who will be living in cities by 2050. The re-birth of the megastructure, an all encompassing framework that can house the functional parts of the city, not only explores porosity by the erosion of the building fabric to create social space, but also the counterbalancing of objects to create the very same.

Figure 62: *Reflections*, Singapore: skycourts link tall buildings and serve as recreational destinations for their inhabitants

Figure 63: *The Interlace*, Singapore: a megastructure that can be viewed as a vertical modernism with the skygardens floating in undifferentiated skyspace

Figure 64: *Acqua Livingstone*, Manila: a lofty, permeable skygarden with an abundance of natural light and ventilation becomes a recreational destination for its occupants

Figure 65: Work from students of the Nottingham University MArch in Sustainable Tall Buildings

Arguably, this can be viewed as the space left over following form creation, and may be conceived spatially as a 'vertical modernism' (Figure 63). This is where counter-poised, object-driven blocks are left freely to float in undifferentiated sky space, and places skycourts and skygardens as secondary to the blocks – thus challenging the idea of containing social space as seen in previous examples.

The works on the drawing board embrace and develop both the concept of the point block tower and the interlinked series of tall buildings as megastructures. This could be in part attributed to population increase, the migration to city centres and the consequent urbanisation, which necessitate an increase in density, scale and multiplicity of uses within developments. This requires a greater ratio of sky-rise social spaces to built-up area. These environments – loftier to permit light and ventilation to percolate deeper inside the floor plates, greener and appropriately orientated to maximise climatic responsiveness, more integrated with circulatory patterns within the tall building to permit an ease of movement, and activated by communal and economic uses to encourage greater social interaction within the development – may well prove to bear more public domain characteristics than its predecessors (Figure 64).

The future city is almost utopian in nature, and arguably once again follows Banham's observations of how the perceived future often has elements of reality that can be found within the existing habitat (Banham, 1976). The visions appear to be unfettered by the realities of today and may be mistaken for being influenced by the celluloid machinations of directors such as Fritz Lang, Ridley Scott or Luc Besson, or the vertical edifices on paper by architects such as Yona Friedman, Archigram or Super Studio. Some of the case studies have demonstrated how the theoretical solutions of students are heavily influenced by the issues that beset the city of tomorrow, and are underpinned by more radical technologies and ideas that seek to address densification, space replenishment, social re-engagement, climate change, fossil fuel depletion, and food and water distribution (Figure 65). The future city therefore must be utopian and challenging to safeguard against complacency and to continue the line of development of how visions can become a reality.

Skycourt/skygarden area to gross floor area (chronological)

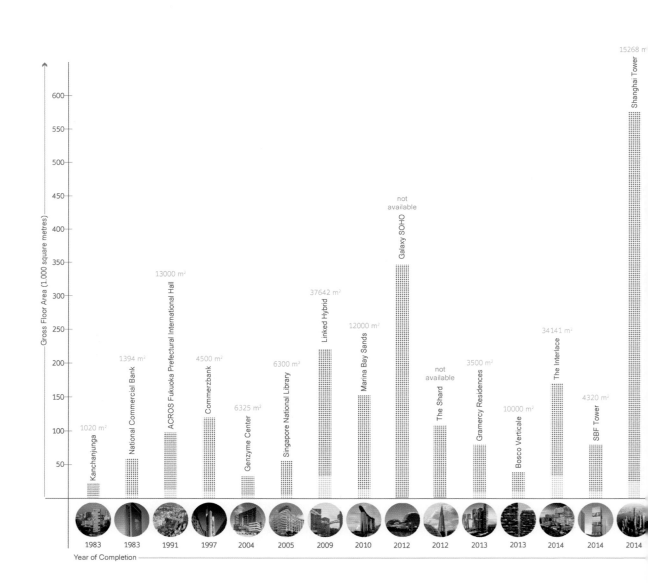

Gross Floor Area (1,000 square metres)

600 —
550 —
500 —
450 —
400 —
350 —
300 —
250 —
200 —
150 —
100 —
50 —

Building	Value	Year
Kanchanjunga	1020 m²	1983
National Commercial Bank	1394 m²	1983
ACROS Fukuoka Prefectural International Hall	13000 m²	1991
Commerzbank	4500 m²	1997
Genzyme Center	6325 m²	2004
Singapore National Library	6300 m²	2005
Linked Hybrid	37642 m²	2009
Marina Bay Sands	12000 m²	2010
Galaxy SOHO	not available	2012
The Shard	not available	2012
Gramercy Residences	3500 m²	2013
Bosco Verticale	10000 m²	2013
The Interlace	34141 m²	2014
SBF Tower	4320 m²	2014
Shanghai Tower	15268 m²	2014

Year of Completion

Gross floor area

Skycourt/skygarden area

Data unavailable for gross floor area

Data unavailable for area of skycourts/skygardens

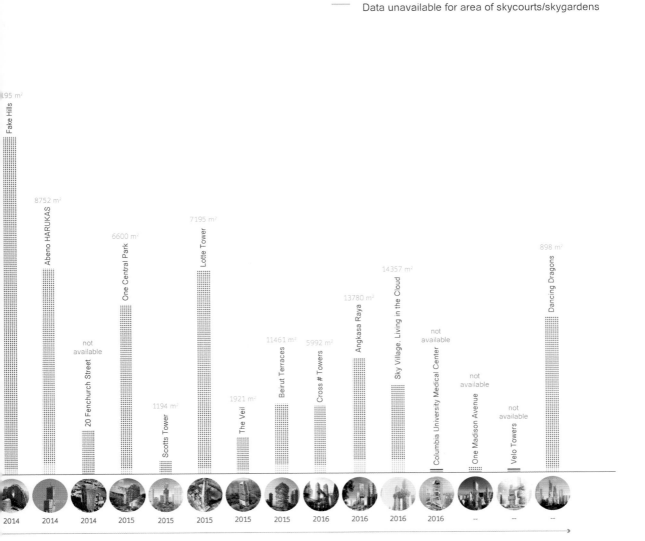

195 m²
Fake Hills

8752 m²
Abeno HARUKAS

not available
20 Fenchurch Street

6600 m²
One Central Park

1194 m²
Scotts Tower

7195 m²
Lotte Tower

1921 m²
The Veil

11461 m²
Beirut Terraces

5992 m²
Cross # Towers

13780 m²
Angkasa Raya

14357 m²
Sky Village. Living in the Cloud

not available
Columbia University Medical Center

not available
One Madison Avenue

not available
Velo Towers

898 m²
Dancing Dragons

2014 2014 2014 2015 2015 2015 2015 2015 2016 2016 2016 2016 -- -- --

Percentage skycourt/skygarden area to gross floor area

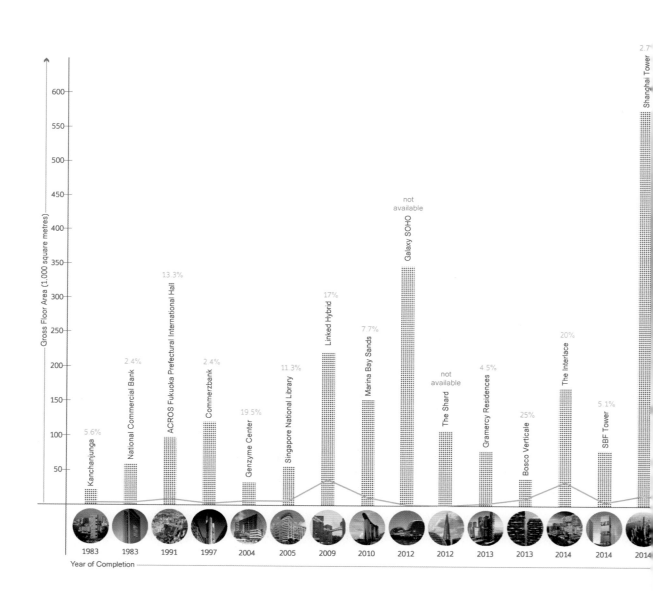

Gross Floor Area (1,000 square metres)

2.7% Shanghai Tower

not available
Galaxy SOHO

13.3%
ACROS Fukuoka Prefectural International Hall

17%
Linked Hybrid

7.7%
Marina Bay Sands

20%
The Interlace

2.4%
National Commercial Bank

2.4%
Commerzbank

11.3%
Singapore National Library

not available
The Shard

4.5%
Gramercy Residences

5.1%
SBF Tower

5.6%
Kanchanjunga

19.5%
Genzyme Center

25%
Bosco Verticale

| 1983 | 1983 | 1991 | 1997 | 2004 | 2005 | 2009 | 2010 | 2012 | 2012 | 2013 | 2013 | 2014 | 2014 | 2014 |

Year of Completion

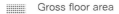 Gross floor area

% of skycourt/skygarden area to gross floor area

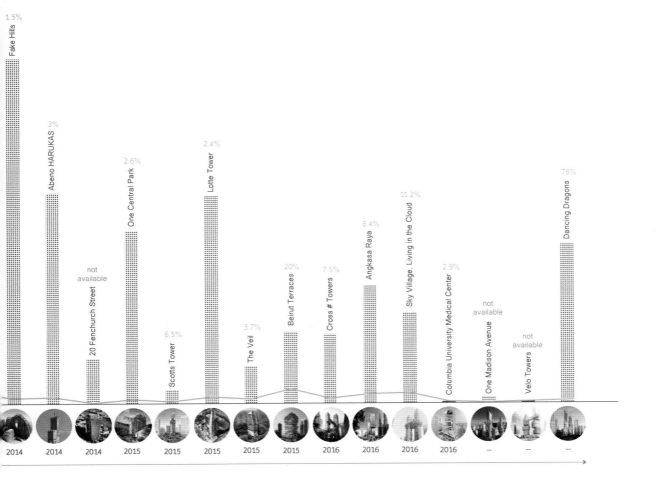

Skycourts/skygardens by geographic location

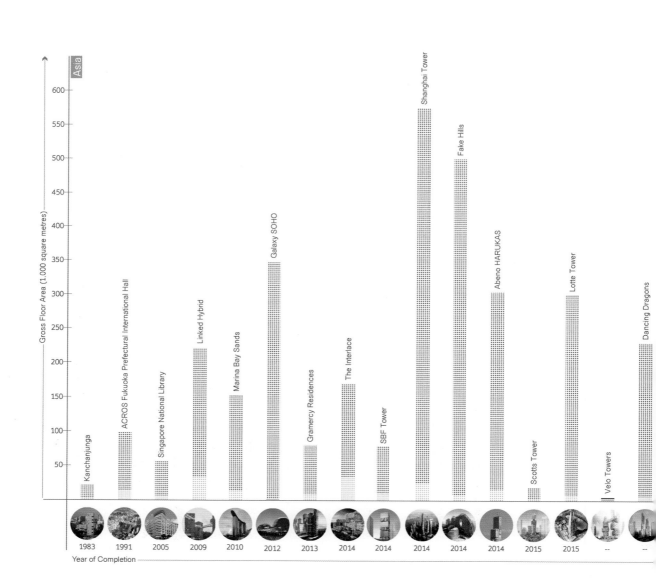

Asia

Gross Floor Area (1,000 square metres)

- Kanchanjunga — 1983
- ACROS Fukuoka Prefectural International Hall — 1991
- Singapore National Library — 2005
- Linked Hybrid — 2009
- Marina Bay Sands — 2010
- Galaxy SOHO — 2012
- Gramercy Residences — 2013
- The Interlace — 2014
- SBF Tower — 2014
- Shanghai Tower — 2014
- Fake Hills — 2014
- Abeno HARUKAS — 2014
- Scotts Tower — 2015
- Lotte Tower — 2015
- Velo Towers — --
- Dancing Dragons — --

Year of Completion

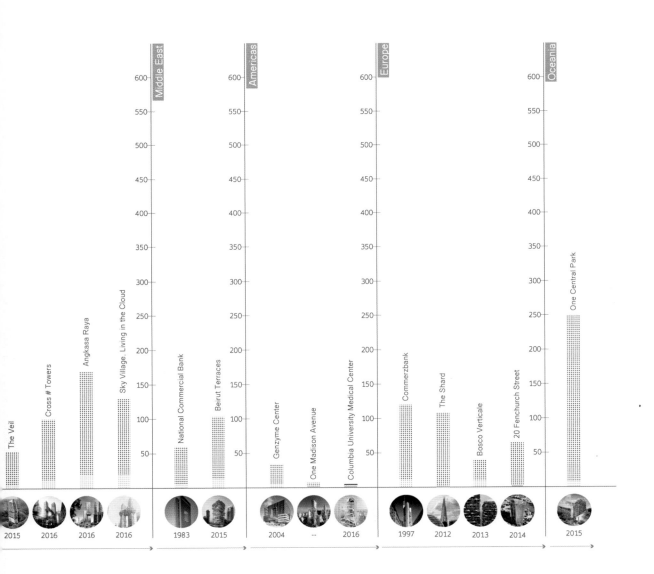

Gross floor area

Skycourt/skygarden area

Skycourts/skygardens space usage

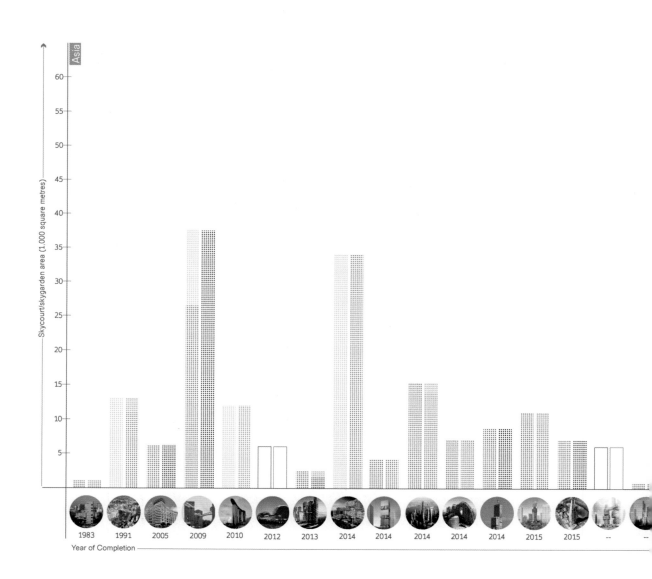

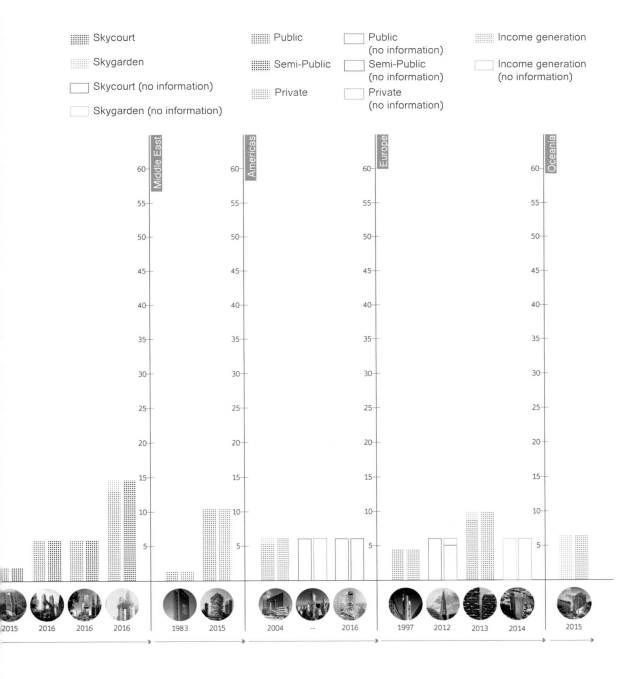

4.2 Sustainable principles to support a vertical urban theory

In 1987, the World Commission on Environment and Development sought to address the concern 'about the accelerating deterioration of the human environment and natural resources, and the consequences of that deterioration for economic and social development' (Brundtland, 1987). It published its findings in *Our Common Future*, and it is from this report that sustainable development was first defined as 'meet[ing] the needs of the present without compromising the ability of future generations to meet their own needs' (Brundtland, 1987). It has been argued that if a development is to be truly sustainable, a balance between the needs of Man and Nature is required through the careful trade-off between social, economic and environmental parameters of equal weighting, which the academic Mark Mawhinney refers to as the balance theory of sustainability (Mawhinney, 2002). Population increase and the need for modernisation in the developing world, coupled with the unsustainable consumption levels in the developed world, pose challenges to the sustainability of future cities, as the ill-gotten mistakes of developed nations pre-Brundtland fail to deter developing nations' quest for economic prosperity. The sustainable city in itself is an oxymoron, given the fact that 50% of global carbon emissions are generated through the built environment, of which 80% are caused by cities. But does the triple bottom line go far enough in addressing such issues in the future?

We have considered the cause and effect of spatial depletion within cities, and the consequent benefits of creating alternative social spaces. We have also considered the cultural transformation of the way in which people perceive, and then interface, with each other in public and semi-public domains. This has been underpinned by a technical/technological understanding of how skycourts and skygardens can socio-economically enhance the user experience aswell as the environmental performance of tall buildings within dense urban habitats. These spatial, cultural and technological considerations are vital if we are to be able to construct people-centred and yet environmentally responsive high-density solutions for the city of tomorrow. In the context of our future urban habitat, a vertical urban theory that embraces just the social, economic and environmental pillars of sustainability may not go far enough in addressing the above issues. It arguably requires these three additional considerations in both the process of design and the realisation of the future city. After all, world population is projected to exceed 9 billion people by 2050. Developing countries will have the biggest growth, with a projected rise from 5.6 billion in 2009 to 7.9 billion in 2050 (OECD, 2012). This will inevitably result in three issues: the heightened social and cultural transmigration as a response to urbanisation and rising land prices; the privatisation of space and the consequent depletion of those environments that once fostered social interaction; and the continued rise in urban temperatures that contribute to climate change. A spatial, cultural and technological sustainability would therefore seem an important set of parameters that should be considered alongside the widely accepted 'triple bottom line' in order to create more robust urban habitats that reinforce the edict of 'people, profit and planet'.

Figure 66: Dining out in Hong Kong can demonstrate spatial constraints through densification

Space, as we have seen, is a commodity in need of preservation and replenishment, and continues to be depleted through urbanisation. One feels conscious of this in high-density environments such as Hong Kong – whether this is through experiencing the compactness of a micro-apartment or even simply sharing a table in a restaurant that has been ergonomically attuned to cater for multiple strangers dining at any one time (Figure 66). Space and society are intrinsically linked, and one cannot have a discourse about society and the way people interact without also discussing the space in which they can do this. If we are to foster a greater sense of community, the ability to consider a spatial sustainability as a counterpoint to social sustainability therefore seems key to the success of our high-density vertical urban habitats in the 21st century, especially as spatial configuration has been found to correlate with social behaviour (Hillier and Hanson, 1984, 1987).

Cultural identity, and particularly that of a people and the environment in which they inhabit, is increasingly becoming challenged through globalisation. Whilst technology has helped bring people together and promoted the cross-fertilisation of cultures, ideas and ideals, it has also contributed to a transcendence of the international corporation and homogenised Western consumer culture that arguably destroys the sense of identity of a people (Tomlinson, 1999). Spaces that were once imprinted with the cultural practices, beliefs and traditions of a local people are also being removed through continued urbanisation, which further compromises the cultural identity of a place (Figure 67). A cultural sustainability that seeks to preserve traditional social and spatial practices potentially safeguards against the imposition of a modern built environment that lacks cultural relevance. Such an approach evokes the academic John Tomlinson's assertions that 'globalization is really the globalization of modernity, and modernity is the harbinger of identity' (Tomlinson, 1999), and suggests that cultural identity may in fact be strengthened in its ability to form a localised counterpoint to globalisation.

Technological advancement may have created as many questions as it has answers, and society's continued use has deeply embedded technology into every part of our everyday life – further fuelling our determination to accomplish lifestyle enhancements and changes. Numerous studies of the social and environmental impacts of new technologies on society show that the effects of a technology depend not just on inherent characteristics of a technology, but especially on the way it is perceived, and used, and its ability to transform the context (Figure 68).

A technological sustainability that acknowledges Ernst Schumacher's idea that technological choice can be small-scale, energy-efficient, environmentally sound, people-centred and locally controlled, permits more community-focused activity (for instance, irrigation systems for rooftop gardens that harvest rainwater) to work in symbiosis with broader city-wide interventions (photovoltaic green roofs that generate solar energy). It is perhaps fitting that we should conclude the benefits of skycourts and skygardens as new social spaces for the 21st century by considering these six parameters, from which we can outline 'prompts for further thinking' for the creation of better skyrise social spaces for the 21st century.

Figure 67: *Clarke Quay*, Singapore: an example of how the old and new can co-exist and in so doing retain the charm and cultural practices of a place

Figure 68: *Academy of Sciences*, California: an example of appropriate technologies being applied to minimise environmental impact

1. If form follows function, object follows space in the new hybrid

Figure 69: A five-foot verandah, Singapore: a sheltered thoroughfare that provides both social space and a transition space in the same instance

The process by which Nolli mapped the city of Rome has left an indelible mark on the way that urban planners and architects conceive and map the physical character of cities. It serves as a tool worthy of consideration in its ability to define what the urbanist Camillo Sitte regarded as the 'outdoor rooms' of social engagement that were formed by the building façades that encapsulated them. The replenishment of space is, in the same instance, an opportunity to replenish cultural identity – whether enabling a family's quiet contemplation within a courtyard space of a Middle Eastern city, a group's experience of traditional festivities within a piazza of a European city, or an individual's ability to traverse through a five-foot verandah of a south-east Asian city (Figure 69). The ability to reinterpret the physical essence of a particular urban habitat, through the study of its spatial morphology, challenges the preconceived notion of the tall building as a self-same, or self-similar, extruded form within the 20th century city of objects, by becoming a 'self-differentiated' form that incorporates social spaces in order to create what we can call the 21st century *hybrid city*.

This is both timely and necessary, as modernisation and urbanisation have seen the imposition of the tall building not just as a means of increasing urban density, but also as a symbol of power over one's peers, and an opportunity for corporations to impart their brand culture. The modern blocks in undifferentiated space are a globalised phenomenon that may not necessarily be differentiated from one location to another, and has challenged the spatio-cultural identity of the city of spaces. The need to preserve the city of spaces (or the 'traditional city'), whilst acknowledging the symbiotic presence of the existing city of objects (or the 'modern city'), requires the careful reinterpretation of the scale, form, height and mass of the existing context, as well as a respect for a people's cultural practices. In so doing, it requires space to be a container of functions as well as society's interaction, and take precedence over the object.

Skycourts and skygardens within the hybrid city support this paradigm shift, and can acknowledge a reinterpretative, as opposed to replicative, approach to open space creation. Their pluralistic nature can potentially evoke the character and grain of the existing city and its public realm as either open or enclosed spaces – depending on the climatic conditions of the place and the environmental strategy of the building that retains them. A hierarchy of void space assists in integrating the hybrid building within the urban fabric. It is analogous to the hierarchical levels of figurative void between the public square and the semi-public court within the 18th century hotel, the arcade within the 19th century galleria or the strip within the 20th century retail mall. Such an approach challenges the preconception of the tall building as a stand-alone object designed from the outside in, and establishes the mixed-use hybrid as a 'vertical city' designed from the inside out.

Spatially mapping the existing grain through figure ground, and even figure section, analysis can therefore provide a starting point for creating familiar scaled spaces for the people who live, work and play, and who were born, grew up and retired in the urban habitat. Simply put, it conceives the tall building within the hybrid city as a three-dimensional, as opposed to a two-dimensional, Nolli diagram rotated in 90 degrees – an environment with skycourts as the new social spaces. A context-specific ratio of open space to built-up area could therefore be employed within the hybrid that is scaled accordingly to further create a hierarchy of spaces that support the larger open spaces of the ground. In plan, it would suggest a similar density more akin with the urban fabric as opposed to the scale of the high-rise.

Alejandro Carrasco and Omelmominin Wadidy's student design project takes inspiration from a spatial vernacular in the Middle East (Figure 70). It draws inspiration from *sikkas* – narrow alleys running between buildings that create comfortable spaces which are shaded from the harsh desert sun and wind, and are suitable for circulation and socio-communal activities that are found in traditional urban developments of the region. Multi-storey stacked sikkas and a series of six-storey courtyards evoke the grain of the traditional context, and act as the social hubs where people can meet and children can come to play in the shade[5].

Figure 70: *Sikkas in the Sky*, Abu Dhabi: a reinterpretation of the traditional urban fabric that is extrapolated vertically through a series of sikkas and skycourts

(5) Interview with Dr. Phil Oldfield, Nottingham University, 2013.

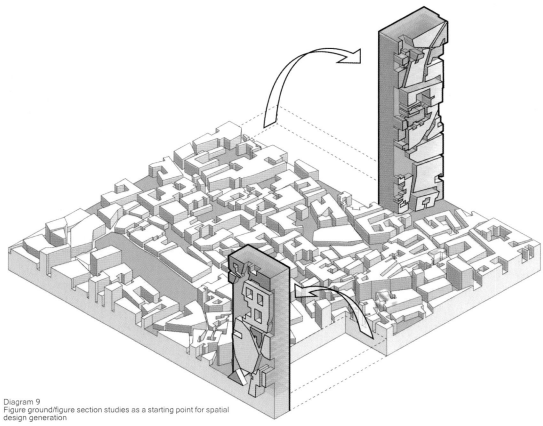

Diagram 9
Figure ground/figure section studies as a starting point for spatial design generation

'Spatially mapping the existing grain through figure ground, and even figure section, analysis can therefore provide a starting point for creating familiar scaled spaces for the people who live, work and play, and who were born, grew up and retired in the urban habitat.'

2. Mixed use becomes 'mixed-up vertical use'

If the traditional city can be viewed as the product of a constant, yet organic, evolutionary process of adapting according to the societal and economic need of the time, then the modern city was the product of a structured, and an almost 'seismic', commercial process. Where the former was reliant on passive systems of harnessing natural light and ventilation, the latter became increasingly reliant on the active artificial systems. And where one was a diverse 'melange' of economic programmes that sought to provide continuity or enclosure to the figurative spaces in which social and economic scenes could take place (for instance, cultural festivals, market days or outdoor performances), the other's diversity can be viewed as a compartmentalised array of uses strictly controlled within social, spatial, functional and time-based boundaries. The former lends itself to a 24-hour social vibrancy of spontaneous interaction, whilst the latter becomes at best pre-scheduled, or at worst ghettoised, environments within given times frames.

'Melange' may be an appropriate word to denote the 'mixing-up' of functional uses and activities in the hybrid city. It challenges the modern city that is often conceived in a two-dimensional plan view and is then represented as different coloured zones that correlate to the different functions of the city. It is an approach that does little to represent the often stratified and disparate uses that can evolve over time, and can take place within high-density urban habitats. Places such as Hong Kong have a myriad of 'mixed-up' uses that are visible in both plan and sectional representation over various super and subterranean levels, which necessitate a three-dimensional assessment of uses (Figure 71). The hybrid city acknowledges the existence of the traditional and the modern, re-assesses its existing use strategies (be they heterogeneous and stratified, or homogeneous extrusions of the same function) and employs a three-dimensional layering of uses and activities that either extrapolates what has already been established within the city or implements new functions and activities to balance the local economy. Such an approach enriches the urban life quality for its inhabitants by identifying activity gaps and then

Figure 71: Hong Kong has a myriad of 'mixed-up' uses that necessitates a three-dimensional assessment of its functions over its multiple super and subterranean levels

vertically adding functions that utilise air space, as opposed to horizontally occupying and depleting ground space.

The tall building within the hybrid city has the potential to become a 24-hour vertical neighbourhood or town which has the dynamic qualities of traditional urban habitats that once permitted people to live, work, play, learn, heal, relax and interact; an environment that organically intertwines all aspects of life in the same vicinity. Such co-presence of a broad demographic of people, co-dependence of uses and intensity through density can help create a sustained vibrancy that ameliorates the risk of ghetto formation and instead fosters a greater sense of community. The skycourt plays a fundamental role in being able to bring these disparate uses together and not only provides a means of passage between one use and another, but becomes a forum that is activated with the presence of shops, cafés, restaurants and other income-generating retail opportunities (Figure 72). This can help draw people through the hybrid and provide further convenience to the intermediary and upper realms of the building that negates the need to travel groundward for the same conveniences at street level. Such an approach can increase footfall and enhance income generation through passing trade, thus creating a more commercially viable retail environment with greater prospects for social interaction through chance meeting. It also enhances revenue generation for both developer and tenant in a fashion reminiscent of the traditional arcade.

With heightened pedestrian footfall and co-presence comes also the potential for skycourts to be used for further third party revenue-generating opportunities, such as event spaces and digital media. The heightened value brought to real estate through the provision of a safe, well-maintained and inclusive high-quality public realm that is conducive to civil society's use can be paralleled by skycourts. Their ability to embody a neutrality can permit different events, performances or trade to take place, and enables the building's adaptation to alternative uses within its life-cycle given shifting social, political or economic influences. With Generation 'Y' being the first to be born into the information age, skycourts can also be used as a media exchange and an additional source of income for the developer at those critical nodes of high footfall (Figure 73). Just as high-density

Figure 72: *World Financial Centre*, Shanghai: the skycourt provides an opportunity for income generation, not least in its function as an observation deck that can levy a fee

Figure 73: Digital media has played an important role as a means of information exchange as well as a tool for one's spatial recognition of the city

environments such as *Times Square*, New York or *Shinjuku*, Tokyo have become landmarks characterised by their advertising, communication and information exchanges through digital media, skycourts can employ the very same, and in the process aid the spatial cognition of the vertical urban habitat.

Arham Daoudi, Chandni Chadha, Elnaz Eidinejad and Akshay Sethi's student design project aims to create a residential-led vertical community with a variety of ancillary uses and activities, which includes a design school on the lower 15 storeys, bound together by aspects of colour and art (Figure 74). Rather than restrict the tower to the blues and greys of typical curtain walling, the design aims to integrate colour and vibrancy by 'mapping' the colours of the surroundings onto each façade. Thus, the south façade takes on the primary colours of the adjacent Container City, the blues and greys of the Thames, the white of the O_2 Dome and the reds, browns and greens of residential communities further south. In this way, each façade reflects the context in which it faces in an abstract manner. Timber louvres on the façade provide shading and privacy to the residents, but also serve to create a dynamic, ever changing elevation as blocks of colour are exposed and hidden as the louvres are opened and closed. At night the façade of the design school is used as a blank canvas to project movies, student work, digital exhibitions and other digital advertising media, further enlivening the experience of the building and enhancing its legibility. This design was the recipient of the 2009/10 Canary Wharf Tall Building Design Award[6].

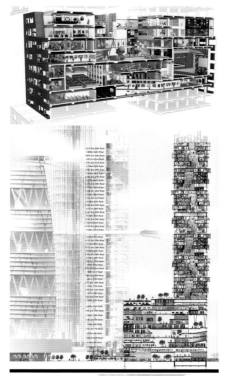

Figure 74: *Colour My Thames*, London: a mixed-use tall building that embraces digital media and colour to bring a 24-hour vibrancy to London

(6) Interview with Dr. Phil Oldfield, Nottingham University, 2013.

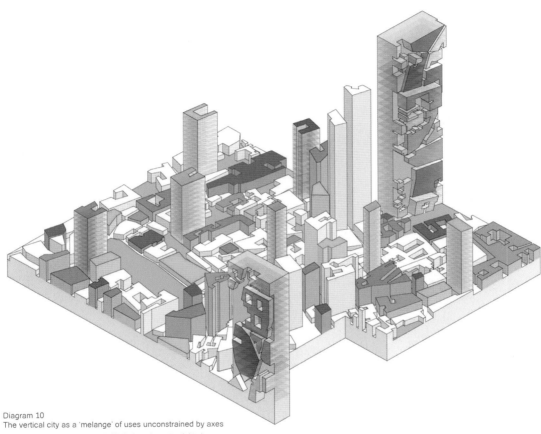

Diagram 10
The vertical city as a 'melange' of uses unconstrained by axes

'The tall building within the hybrid city has the potential to become a 24-hour vertical neighbourhood or town which has the dynamic qualities of traditional urban habitats that once permitted people to live, work, play, learn, heal, relax and interact; an environment that organically intertwines all aspects of life in the same vicinity.'

3. Movement is the social gel

The design of skycourts and their spatial requirements can be further defined by using more quantitative methods, such as space syntax, as a means of predicting patterns of pedestrian movement in order to enhance social co-presence through the hybrid city. Space syntax has proven that spatial configuration correlates with aggregate pedestrian movement, and can explain its variance in different locations, be that in urban or building spaces (Hillier *et al.* 1993; Peponis *et al.* 1989). It quantifies aspects of social pattern without reference to the individual's motivation, origin/destination, land use or density, scale, height and massing, or other prompts that may bear influence. In so doing, it provides a mechanism for a predictive theory of mass movement based on rational choices of the individuals' spatial cognition. Pedestrian movement has similarly been found to correlate with spatial integration (i.e. an area's predictability), which in itself is correlated to the degree of intelligibility of an area. Hillier identified the intelligibility of space as the integration of primary and secondary routes and the pedestrians' cognitive understanding of the space. The greater the spatial integration, the greater the potential for main integrating axes to be frequented by pedestrians; and in turn the more intelligible the spaces/axes. Conversely, as spaces/axes become less intelligible, the correlation between spatial integration and movement is compromised, resulting in the axes potentially being sparsely frequented by pedestrians (Figure 75).

Tall buildings have been found to have a poor correlation between spatial integration and movement – their intelligibility breaking down over a series of multiple layers. The position of the vertical access, be that lift, ramp, stairs or elevator, are usually deep plan – several steps removed from the main integrating (and therefore highly trafficked) axis. This leads to lower levels of visual accessibility and intelligibility of the space. Skycourts may not always provide the opportunity to pause, observe and orientate, and repetitive floor plate configurations also negate the visual diversity that often helps people orientate themselves. If intelligible urban spaces are those which correlate spatial configuration with movement and forward visibility, skycourts could be similarly configured

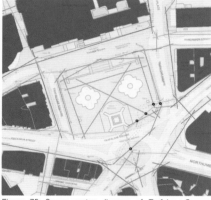

Figure 75: Space syntax diagram of *Trafalgar Square*, London: space syntax has proven that spatial configuration correlates with aggregate pedestrian movement

to facilitate an ease of movement in order to release their potential as transitional urban spaces in the sky that have heightened intelligibility and opportunities for spontaneous social interaction through chance meeting.

Undertaking space syntax analysis to facilitate the design of skycourts places movement and space at the core of the design process. It can be used as a predictive theory of mapping pedestrian behaviour to diagnose spatial/ movement deficiencies in skycourts within tall buildings. Modelling in three dimensions the vertical, diagonal and horizontal circulation allows for space to be shaped for a greater freedom of pedestrian movement in the sky. Using space syntax can also improve the design by identifying 'supporting' spaces within the skycourt that could be used for rest and recuperation, observation, refreshment, events, meetings and social interaction (Figure 76).

Due consideration would need to be given to a range of variables to axially map the spatial configuration and its movement three-dimensionally. This would suggest that for space syntax to be a useful predictive tool, the vertical, horizontal and diagonal means of circulation (the travellators, lifts, ramps, staircases) will need to be included in the calculation, but weighted to reflect their public, semi-public or private designation. Passenger capacity of any mechanical mode of transport would also need to be calculated (the lift car for example) to ascertain similar pedestrian flows from ground level to and from the skycourt and beyond (Gabay and Aravot, 2003; Pusharev and Zupan, 1975; Pomeroy 2008). The hybrid city's connectivity with skyway or concourse systems would also necessitate the modelling of parking structures, the metro and other auxiliary systems (not normally considered part of the urban grid in axial models) if one was to truly understand movement patterns through the public and semi-public spaces on the ground, and through to the skycourts within their respective tall buildings.

As more super high-rise schemes are developed over 80 storeys, the ability to link with other structures for structural and simultaneous evacuation strategies will increase, which in turn will necessitate advanced lifting strategies to be integrated within their respective sky transfer lobbies to

Figure 76: *Pompidou Centre*, Paris: its external escalator demonstrates an alternative means of vertical circulation that permits visual connection to the urban habitat

facilitate an ease of vertical and diagonal movement. Once these mechanised means of circulation are incorporated into the model, and the obstacle of floor plate separation is overcome, a rethinking of how to assess movement vertically by employing space syntax through three dimensions will become essential, as two-dimensional axial mapping will no longer be sufficient.

David Calder, Matthew Bryant and Amrita Chowdhury's student design project for Leamouth, London demonstrates a new realm in the sky that is facilitated by skybridges that further permit an ease of movement. Rather than focusing on the design of a single tower, the students in this group were responsible for developing the masterplan beyond a strategic level by designing in detail the skybridges and groundscraper. The result is the creation of a new urban vision for Leamouth (Figure 77). The groundscraper is conceived as an extension to the Lea Valley 'green corridor', tying the site into its surroundings. A new public realm is envisaged on a site-wide habitable green roof, with all the building services and parking located below at 'ground' level. A skybridge network is created at height between the towers, lifting the public domain into the sky and connecting all the key public facilities within the buildings. Each tower has specific public transportation linking the ground-floor interface with the skybridge network above, through shuttle elevators, escalators or ramped green pathways. The skybridges are designed as modular units that can be easily assembled on site, with prefabricated 'retail pods' suspended along their length. The northern-most skybridge includes a large green roof, creating a public skypark some 200 metres above the city that seeks to replenish social space for the towers' occupants. In the same instance, it permits an additional circulatory route that provides a greater freedom of movement through choice[7].

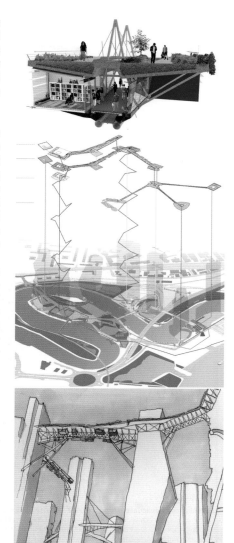

Figure 77: *Leamouth Linked Towers*, London: exploring the skybridge as a means of enhancing movement whilst providing recreational and community support facilities

(7) Interview with Dr. Phil Oldfield, Nottingham University, 2013.

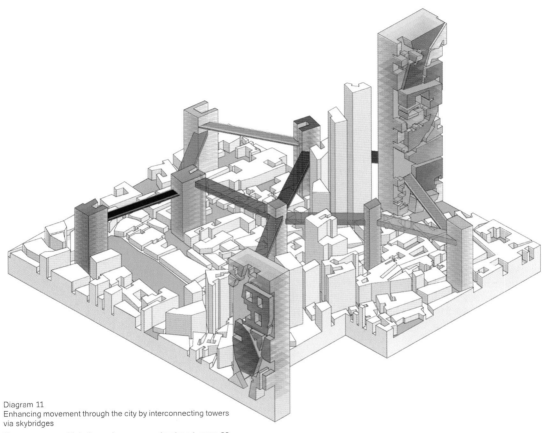

Diagram 11
Enhancing movement through the city by interconnecting towers
via skybridges

'As more super high-rise schemes are developed over 80
storeys, the ability to link with other structures for structural
and simultaneous evacuation strategies will increase, which in
turn will necessitate advanced lifting strategies to be integrated
within their respective sky transfer lobbies to facilitate an ease of
vertical and diagonal movement.'

4. Technological and technical considerations in a vertical urban realm

The densification of our cities has not only spawned the creation of a new hybrid city comprised of mixed-use structures and their social spaces, but also the sustainable democratisation of existing rooftop spaces and their air rights. In Hong Kong, where less than 25% of its 1,104 kilometres of land surface area is developable, the physical constraints of a steep and rocky terrain and marshland impose high urban densities of 29,400 persons per square kilometre, making it one of the densest cities in the world (Ng, 2010). With high housing prices, illegal rooftop structures that do not comply with the planning or building control process continue to be the homes of 3,962 ethnic Chinese (95.5%), Indian, Pakistani, Filipino and Nepalese (4.5%) illegal immigrants who have salaries below the median household level of the territory of HK$10,000, or US$1,282 (HKSAR 2008). The now demolished *Kowloon Walled City* aptly demonstrated how such illegal extensions were the home of an underprivileged and marginalised sector who faced social difficulties integrating into an otherwise affluent Hong Kong community (Sinn, 1987; Chui, 2008) (Figure 78).

Figure 78: *Kowloon Walled City*, Hong Kong: an example of illegal rooftop extension that became home to a marginalised sector of society

Such issues of densification through rooftops and air rights have, however, also been explored legally. In the Netherlands, 1.9 million of the 3.4 million hectares of land surface area (or 55.8%) is designated for income-generating agricultural produce that impinges on the opportunity of satellite urbanism (Sukkel *et al.*, 2009). The 'topping-up' of rooftops in the Netherlands has therefore been explored in both research and commercial projects, and has consequently created a new skyward architectural realm that seeks to increase urban density without necessarily demolishing and re-building the existing urban fabric to achieve greater plot ratios (Melet and Vreedenburgh, 2005). Projects such as *The Bridge* in Rotterdam aptly demonstrate this, and how the topping-up expansion of rooftop properties can be considered further as a legally acceptable means of increasing the density in our cities (Figure 79). However, whilst legitimising the exploitation of rooftop space and

Figure 79: *The Bridge*, Rotterdam: an example of the legal exploitation of air rights to increase urban densities

air rights may prove an alternative, there are a number of issues that are both socially and physically challenging in the generic European city. Preservationist by-laws reduce the built fabric's ability for functional change in addition to their very physical structures being less likely to include further programmes of accommodation through structural adaptation above the roof level. Furthermore, issues of access may reduce the efficiency of the building and may make retro-fitting expensive, particularly if different uses are 'topped' above another that would necessitate separate vertical access.

Nevertheless, post-colonial cities that went through a process of demolishing and re-building (thus having structures potentially newer and more capable for rooftop topping-up) may provide opportunities for such an application. Singapore, like Hong Kong, is faced with the spatial constraint of being an island. With an urban density of 8,350 persons per kilometre and an increasing population that is set to grow from 4.98 million people in 2010 to 5.5 million people by 2050[8], the need to house an increase in population has seen ever increasing plot ratios in urban areas and the costly demolition of existing structures to facilitate higher densities. However, should an existing housing development retain a certain structural integrity, and the infrastructure in place caters for localised vertical extension, the ability to create rooftop architecture could be a viable alternative to demolishing and re-building (Figure 80). This would make the exploitation of air rights and rooftop spaces an additional solution to the densification of city centres by making use of existing energy systems, maximising existing public infrastructure and helping reduce the pressure to develop on open spaces.

Technological considerations of enhancing the structural and services infrastructure of the existing rooftops need to also be balanced with technical guidelines to facilitate the delivery of ideas for a new vertical urban realm. Technical guidelines that also control the design, construction and maintenance of skycourts, skygardens and their vertical infrastructure should be reinforced by legislation that ensures a minimum provision of open space to built-up area as a pre-requisite to securing planning permission. Such an approach legally seeks to readdress the loss of public space from the

Figure 80: *Blue Cross Blue Shield HQ*, Illinois: an example of 'top-up' architecture, whereby footprints are optimised via the vertical extension of existing structures

(8) www.singstat.gov.sg

ground through local development planning policies, or as contributions to the local government/borough/city in the form of public/private agreements that replenish habitable, social public space in the sky. Legislation could also cede responsibility for such skyrise spaces to public authorities in a fashion not dissimilar to how the streets, pavements and buried services at ground level are financed and maintained by tax-funded bodies and services.

Fei Qian's student design project for a series of car-parking structures in the city aims to address the environmental problems associated with the excessive use of private fossil fuel-powered cars (Figure 81). Inspired by Masdar City's proposals for all-electric autonomous pod cars, it envisions an Abu Dhabi of the future where this scheme has been extended city-wide and residents make their daily travels by using vehicles from a number of huge vertical car pools. The tower itself acts as one such car pool, accommodating 200 apartments and 750 vehicles which are parked using three automated platforms located in the central atria. This vertical parking strategy would provide maximum parking density for the city, freeing up the hundreds of unshaded ground-level car parks that currently litter Abu Dhabi for future building development, thus creating a denser more concentrated city. In addition, the tower also provides the energy for all the cars through the integration of 19,000 square metres of photovoltaic panels on the south, east and west façades, making the most of the high solar incidence in the Middle East. These panels also serve to shade the north-facing apartments and the dramatic full-height central atrium where residents, scientists and visitors alike would watch the automated car-parking process occur[9].

Figure 81: *Solar Parking*, Abu Dhabi: an automated car-parking structure that integrates photovoltaic cells as a citywide energy generator

(9) Interview with Dr. Phil Oldfield, Nottingham University, 2013.

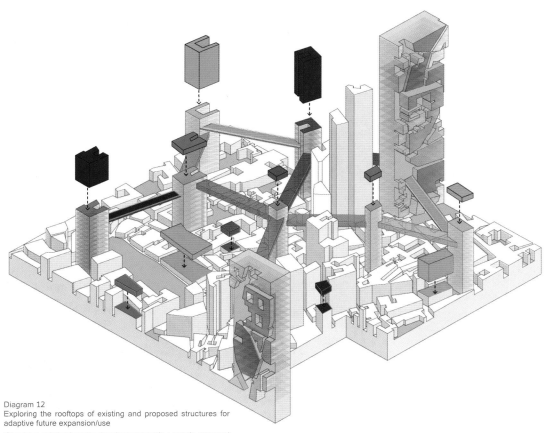

Diagram 12
Exploring the rooftops of existing and proposed structures for adaptive future expansion/use

'Should an existing housing development retain a certain structural integrity, and the infrastructure in place caters for localised vertical extension, the ability to create rooftop architecture could be a viable alternative to demolishing and re-building. This would make the exploitation of air rights and rooftop spaces an additional solution to the densification of city centres.'

5. Greening our urban habitat via more quantifiable means

Cities of the future will be faced with not only having to reduce urban temperatures and provide habitable alternative social spaces that can foster community, but with also having to provide a food source that can help sustain a global population that is set to increase from 6.4 billion people in 2012 to 9.2 billion people in 2050 (UNFPA, 2007). Whilst the land surface area currently dedicated to agricultural produce can meet current food demand today, we will need to find approximately 109 hectares of new land (about 20% more land than is represented by the country of Brazil) to cater for the increase in global population (Despommier and Ellingsen, 2008). As existing vegetated open areas are potentially being depleted through urbanisation, the need to green urban habitats that explore diagonal and vertical planted planes will become essential to provide space for biodiversity, food production, heat and rain interception and pollution mitigation.

Urban farming and the exploitation of the existing rooftops for agricultural production will be increasingly accompanied by vertical urban farms that could be located in under-utilised parts of the city. These could act as catalysts for regeneration whilst providing year-round, organic food production. The urbanisation of agriculture eradicates the need for pesticides and fertilisers and allows farmland to return to nature, thus helping restore ecosystems. Such an approach also reduces the risk of weather-related crop failure given the controlled internal conditions made possible by vertical farming, and can reduce fossil fuel use by negating the need for agricultural machinery and shipping. By-products from the farming process, such as methane generation, can also be used as alternative sources of energy to sustain local community energy need (Figure 82). Depending on the crop, 1 indoor acre can be the equivalent to 4–6 outdoor acres, thus helping decentralise food production, and immediately sustaining the local community (Despommier and Ellingsen, 2008).

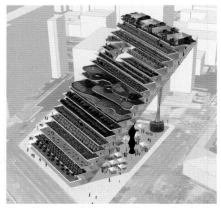

Figure 82: *Locavore Fantasia*, New York: a vertical farming project that incorporates migrant farmers' housing within the stepped terrace design, as well as a farmers' market below

Whilst these factors go some way in balancing social, economic and environmental parameters with the cultural and spatial intricacies of the future city, a more quantifiable and tectonic approach to planting can ensure that the adverse climatic effects of high-density development can be both measured and then mitigated.

The *green plot ratio* can address this issue by assigning numerical values to particular plants based on the surface area of greenery. This is achieved by adapting the leaf area index (LAI) – a biological parameter used to monitor the ecological health of natural ecosystems and to mathematically model and predict metabolic processes (Ong, 2003). For instance, a hypothetical site that has 12 trees and an abundance of turf (and therefore a particular green plot ratio value) may be developed and could lead to the removal of the said quantum of greenery. By assigning values to different types of planting, the ability to replenish the same 'green value' of the 12 trees and turf by alternative means (for instance, shrubs and green walls across the vertical or diagonal surfaces) will ensure a balance of leaf area is retained on the site, and its correlating social, economic and environmental benefits. As such, it can be used as a quantifiable planning metric in biological terms, and consequently provide values of water retention, carbon sequestration or air pollution reduction. It can also be used to measure the level of heat island effect reduction, the absorption of heat in the building fabric and its subsequent re-radiation given the variable environmental properties of different planting types.

Turf, palm, shrubs and trees are the major groups that each have an assigned green plot ratio value based on the leaf area index. Turf has the lowest green plot ratio, as the leaf area index of a blade of grass is less than that of the other categories. Despite trees being larger structures, their leaf area index is still less than a shrub, which has the greatest density of leaf coverage, which in turn has the highest leaf area index. The integration of planting into the design of skycourts and skygardens within the hybrid city provides a balance between the man-made and natural environment, and by employing the green plot ratio as a 'kit of parts', provides a tectonic approach to harnessing its environmental benefits based on 'per square metre' planting modules that could have correlating green plot ratio values, costs and environmental performance measures (Figure 83).

Figure 83: The *green plot ratio:* a quantifiable planning metric in biological terms that assigns values to turf, palms, shrubs and trees based on the leaf area index

Ultimately, this provides a vision for more objective sustainable designs that balance architectural and landscape design within the urban habitat (Figure 84).

Matthew Humphreys' student design project for a series of vertical farms in Singapore considers food sustainability and vertical agriculture within a high-density urban habitat. The city-state is highly dependent on imports for feeding its growing population, with 97% of all food coming from abroad, and just over 1% of the total land mass of the country being devoted to agriculture. The design itself consists of an elongated tower, with the longest sides facing east–west for maximum solar exposure to promote growing. At the northern and southern ends, apartments are located for the farmers. The central parts of the tower consist of an ETFE-clad atrium housing aquaponic-growing systems for the production of fish and food; fish in the tanks produce ammonia-rich waste, much of which is toxic so must be removed. Bacteria in the fish tanks break the ammonia down to nitrates, which is taken in as food by the plants via their roots. This process filters the water as well as fertilising the plants. Fish are then smoked in special smoking towers, the full height of the building. Structurally, the tower is lifted off the ground on large composite structural legs, which opens up the ground floor to be used as a vibrant shaded market[10].

Figure 84: *Vertical Farming*, Singapore: the tower as a food generator that can help sustain the local community

(10) Interview with Dr. Phil Oldfield, Nottingham University, 2013.

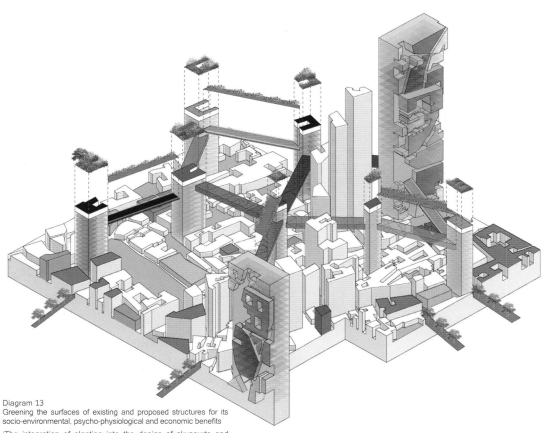

Diagram 13
Greening the surfaces of existing and proposed structures for its
socio-environmental, psycho-physiological and economic benefits

'The integration of planting into the design of skycourts and
skygardens within the hybrid city provides a balance between
the man-made and natural environment, and by employing the
green plot ratio as a "kit of parts", provides a tectonic approach
to harnessing its environmental benefits based on "per square
metre" planting modules that could have correlating green plot
ratio values, costs and environmental performance measures.'

6. The culture of (hybrid) cities

Cultural identity, whether born out of ethnicity, age, gender, nationality or sexual preference, requires a forum in which cultural 'scenes' can be developed through a people's bonds of association which, in the same instance, can help shape the public realm. Just as a theatrical performance may have a variety of plots, subplots and changing scenes that are enriched during the passing of a narrative, so too has the city a variety of changing cultural scenes that are created, altered, strengthened and disbanded by groups through space and time (Blum, 2003). Such scenes, such as the *Palio* in the *Campo* in Siena, are enriched through the passing of time and are constantly negotiated through the predominance of one culture over another. They potentially imprint themselves into the fabric of a city and help define the culture of a place (Figure 85).

The culture of a traditional city and its people has flourished beyond the square as the focal point of public debate and expression of identity, though the remnants of past cultures, and the spaces that were shaped by them, bear influence on the present. The quest for the 'antiquated' or 'authentic' celebrates old buildings, preserved open spaces, markets and old family-owned shops, which, according to the academic Sharon Zukin, educated urbanites and transient tourists crave in their experience of the city (Zukin, 2011). Whether it is Cerda's octagonal courtyard blocks in Barcelona or Haussmann's linear boulevards in Paris, the ability to define a spatial as well as a social culture of a place permits distinct and memorable identities to be preserved for the betterment of current and future generations.

The traditional city often co-exists with the modern city – the preservation of the former permitting tourism that celebrates history and nostalgia for those seeking culture from a place. Its public spaces are often associated with the civic, religious or cultural places and practices of antiquity, and embody what can be deemed the authentic. The library, the church, the museum or the cultural festival are just some of the typologies or happenings that take place. On the other hand, the culture of the modern city may not

Figure 85: *The Palio*, Siena: such traditions enrich the culture of a place into the fabric of the city

necessarily embody the antiquated. In this scenario, Zukin suggests that museums, retail environments, theme parks and restaurants are the new 'public spaces of modernity'. Whilst contributing to a city's cultural gentrification, they show how a predominant private sector economic power can assert its own culture over others, and in so doing, reshape the built environment for the purposes of social, as well as public space, control (Zukin 1996). Replicating the public spaces and their functions from the past, born out of an evolutionary socio-economic and cultural process that can take centuries, as opposed to decades, to form, may not be the answer to forging cultural identity. Such replication may neither foster 'authenticity', nor respond to our current generation's embracing of technology or its increasing acceptance of globalised popular culture that need not require physical co-presence with others but can be satisfied with a virtual co-presence in public. A respect for the essence of a people's traditional and contemporary social practices within the spaces is however something that could be considered.

Najla Gunnur, Soha Hirbod and Fahimeh Soltani's student design project draws inspiration from the 500-year-old vernacular urban precedent of Shibam, Yemen (Figure 86). Known often as the 'Manhattan of the Desert', Shibam is a magnificent walled city of mud towers, some rising up to 11 storeys high, with labyrinth-like alleyways and shaded courtyards below. The design responds to the harsh local climate and reinterprets the historic typology in a modern and contemporary manner. The result is a series of solid, slender towers, clustered around open, yet shaded, courtyards. Alleyways provide circulation without interfering with internal views, thus maintaining occupant privacy – an important consideration in the region. Carved into the mass of the buildings are skycourts, orientated towards the adjacent Gulf for the best views and to harness sea breezes. Rooftop skygardens are created as additional places for play, social interaction and kite flying[11].

At this juncture, the likelihood of a paradigm shift in seeing spaces in the sky, along with their vertical and diagonal circulatory methods, being surrendered entirely to the state seems highly unlikely. What is realistic is the ability to foster greater public domain characteristics if these alternative social spaces are conceived from the outset as new cultural

Figure 86: *A New Shibam*, Yemen: a cultural sensitivity to high-rise design that seeks to reinterpret the 500-year-old walled city of mudtowers

(11) Interview with Dr. Phil Oldfield, Nottingham University, 2013.

foci. This certainly needs tempering. Ceding too much responsibility to the large corporations, groups or individuals, in their continued patronage of cultural activities, could potentially allow them to dictate what is deemed to be culturally relevant to an increasingly culture-consuming society; whilst an overt public intervention could potentially lead to a sterility and even spatial redundancy. A greater symbiosis between public and private interests in the design process, and in the management thereafter, is therefore needed to ensure that culture is not a homogenous representation of just a corporation, group, individual or state's beliefs. It implies a marriage between public and private interests in a similar fashion to the land owner's philanthropic submission of space and social programmes to the city.

Skycourts and skygardens provide a perfect forum for semi-public space creation that can be surrendered for cultural good. By their very presence within the new hybrid, they can become public beacons and focal points for interaction. They could include museums, galleries and even religious settings and other civic functions, in a fashion not too dissimilar to the incorporation of many such elements that contribute to the life of the street and square that they fringe (Figure 87). They seek to be the new 'public space of modernity' in the sky, and embrace the reality of being privatised constructs that are seismic creations that intertwine civil society and state interests.

The most successful public spaces, according to Peter G Rowe, 'have been born out of the shared values of civil society and state, where citizens can engage in public activities and debate among themselves, as well as with the state about matters of public interest ... at the best of times there is often a convergence of these interests, as numerous institutions and other entities find something in common across the boundaries that usually separate the state and civil society, and therefore are in a position to create something civic' (Rowe, 1997). With the increasing democratisation of skycourts and skygardens empowered through governmental legislation, perhaps their adoption within or on top of the private object supports the symbiosis between private and public interests, represented by civil society and state respectively, and will help democratise skycourts and skygardens for greater civic appropriation within the hybrid city of the 21st century.

Figure 87: *Sliced Porosity Block*, Chengdu: the skycourt as a new cultural focus that embraces civil society and state interests

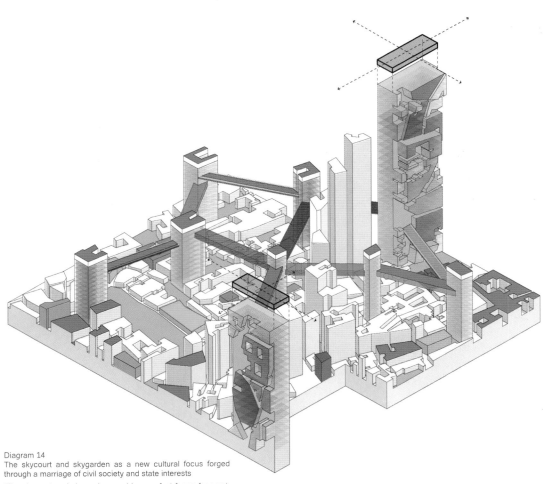

Diagram 14
The skycourt and skygarden as a new cultural focus forged through a marriage of civil society and state interests

'The skycourt and skygarden provide a perfect forum for semi-public space creation that can be surrendered for cultural good. By their very presence within the new hybrid, they can become public beacons and focal points for interaction.'

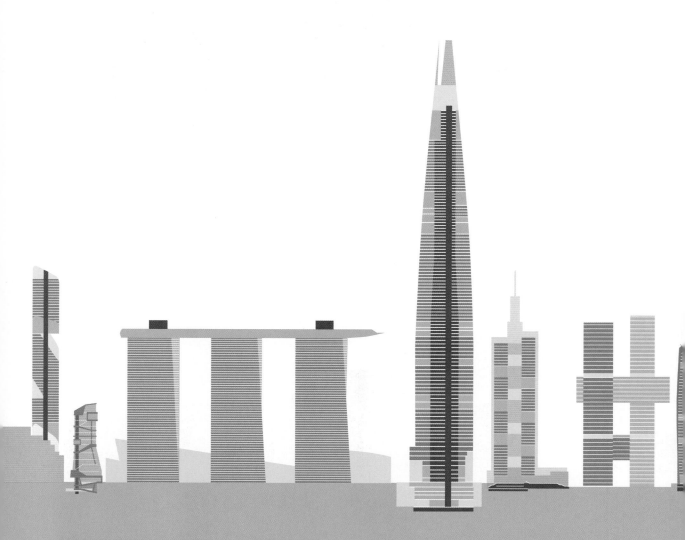

About the author

Prof. Jason Pomeroy is an award-winning architect, masterplanner and academic at the forefront of the sustainable built environment agenda. He graduated with distinction from Canterbury School of Architecture and Cambridge University, and is the founding Principal of Pomeroy Studio. His previous award-winning projects have transcended scale and discipline and included the Idea House, the first carbon zero prototype house in South East Asia; Trump Tower Manila, the tallest residential tower in the Philippines; and Vision Valley Malaysia, an 80,000-acre Network Garden City extension of Kuala Lumpur. In addition to leading the design and research direction of Pomeroy Studio, he lectures internationally and publishes widely. He is the author of *Idea House: Future Tropical Living Today* and is a Professor at the University of Nottingham. He also sits on the editorial board of the Council on Tall Buildings and Urban Habitat.

Image credits

Page 39 Figure 26: Commerzbank Tower, © Andreas Hoffman (http://www.flickr.com/ photos/124330160/4270064950/ in/photostream/)

Page 40 Figure 27: Parisian neighbourhood density, © Mike Poscablo; Figure 28: A Hong Kong neighbourhood, © Jason Pomeroy

Page 41 Figure 29: Mirador Skycourt, © Rob't Hart, Courtesy of MVRDV; Figure 30: Marina Barrage Roof Garden, © Chloe Li

Page 42 Figure 31: (top–bottom) Linked Hybrid, © Shu He, Courtesy of Steven Holl Architects

Page 43 Diagram 1, 1a, 1b, 1c, 1d, 1e, 1f: Skycourt and skygarden spatial morphology, © Pomeroy Studio

Page 44 Figure 32: The South Bank Arts Complex, London, © Veronica Barrett; Figure 33: Ssamziegil, © Jason Pomeroy

Page 45 Figure 34: Sky Garden house rules, © An Anh Nguyen

Page 46 Figure 35: (top–bottom) The Pinnacle, © Philip Oldfield

Page 47 Diagram 2, 2a, 2b, 2c, 2d, 2e, 2f: The skycourt as a social space, © Pomeroy Studio

Page 48 Figure 36: Central mid-level escalators, © Jason Pomeroy; Figure 37: Taipei 101 transfer floor, © Cathy Yang

Page 49 Figure 38: Selfridges bridge link, © Jason Pomeroy

Page 50 Figure 39: (top) The Shard, London, © Michael Denancé, 2012; (bottom) The Shard Viewing Gallery, © Sellar

Page 51 Diagram 3, 3a, 3b, 3c, 3d: The skycourt as a transitional space, © Pomeroy Studio

Page 52 Figure 40: Allen Lambert Galleria, © Jason Pomeroy; Figure 41: Acros Building, Fukuoka, © Hiromi Watanabe – Watanabe Studios, Courtesy of Emilio Ambasz Associates

Page 53 Figure 42: Orchard Central, © An Anh Nguyen

Page 54 Figure 43: (top–bottom) Singapore National Library, © Arham Daoudi

Page 55 Diagram 4, 4a, 4b, 4c, 4d, 4e, 4f: The skycourt and skygarden as an environmental filter, © Pomeroy Studio

Page 56 Figure 44: Pinnacle@Duxton Rooftop, © Jason Pomeroy

Page 57 Figure 45: Genzyme Center Atrium, © Genzyme Corporation; Figure 46: Venice-Mestre Hospital, © Enrico Cano, Courtesy of Emilio Ambasz Associates.

Page 58 Figure 47: (top–bottom) Bedok Court, © An Anh Nguyen

Page 59 Diagram 5, 5a, 5b, 5c, 5d: The skycourt and skygarden enhancing psycho-physiological well-being, © Pomeroy Studio

Page 60 Figure 48: PF-1, © Alexandra Crosby

Page 61 Figure 49: Solaris Research Centre, © Jason Pomeroy; Figure 50: The Highline, © Iwan Baan

Page 62 Figure 51: (top) Overhead view of Supertrees, © Ardison Garcia; (middle–bottom), © Saijel Taank

Bibliography

Alexandri, E. and Jones, P. (2008). 'Temperature decreases in an urban canyon due to green walls and green roofs in diverse climates', in *Building and Environment*, vol. 43, no. 4, April, pp480–493

Arnfield, A.J., Herbert, J.M. and Johnson, G.T. (1999). 'Urban canyon heat source and sink strength variations: a simulation–based sensitivity study', in *Congress of Biometeorology and International Conference on Urban Climate*, WMO, Sydney

Baker, N. and Steemers, K. (2000). *Energy and Environment in Architecture: A Technical Guide*, London: Taylor & Francis

Ballard, J.G. (2003). *High Rise*, London: Flamingo

Banham, R. (1976). *Megastructure: Urban Futures of the Recent Past*, New York: Harper & Row

Banham, R. (1984). *The Architecture of the Well-Tempered Environment*, Chicago: University of Chicago Press

Barghusen, J.D. and Moulder, B. (2001). *Daily Life in Ancient and Modern Cairo*, Minnesota: Twenty-First Century Books

Bay, J.H. (2004). 'Sustainable community and environment in tropical Singapore high rise housing: the case of Bedok Court condominium', in *Architectural Research Quarterly*, vol. 8, no. 3/4, pp333–343

Behrens-Abouseif, D. (1992). *Islamic Architecture in Cairo*, Leiden: Brill Academic Publishers

Best, U. and Struver, A. (2002). *The politics of place: critical of spatial identities and critical spatial identities*, Tokyo: International Critical Geography Group

Betsky, A. (2005). 'Preface' in *Rooftop Architecture*, eds Melet, E. and Vreedenburgh, E., Rotterdam: NAI Publishers, pp7–8

Blum, A.F. (2003). *The Imaginative Structure of the City*, Montreal: McGill-Queen's Press

Burge, P.S. (2004). 'Sick Building Syndrome', in *Occupational and Environmental Medicine*, vol. 61, no. 2, pp185–190

Cheng, V. (2010). 'Understanding density and high density', in *Designing High-Density Cities for Social and Environmental Sustainability*, ed. Ng, E., London: Earthscan, pp3–17

Chiang, K. and Tan, A. (2009). *Vertical Greenery for the Tropics*, Singapore: National Parks Board

Chui, E. (2008). 'Rooftop housing in Hong Kong: an introduction', in *Portraits from Above: Hong Kong's Informal Rooftop Communities*, eds Wu, R. and Canham, S., Berlin: Peperoni Books, pp246–259

Commission for Architecture and the Built Environment (2007). *Guidance on Tall Buildings*, London: CABE

Council on Tall Buildings and Urban Habitat (2011). 'The tallest 20 in 2020: entering the era of the megatall' in *CTBUH Press Release*, December, pp1–7

Council on Tall Buildings and Urban Habitat (2012). 'Tall buildings in numbers', in *CTBUH Journal*, no. 1, pp36–38

Currie, B.A. and Bass, B. (2010). 'Using green roofs to enhance biodiversity in the City of Toronto', a discussion paper prepared for Toronto City Planning, Toronto, Canada

Daley, R.M. and Johnson, S. (2008). 'Chicago: building a green city', in *Congress Proceedings, Tall and Green: Typology for a Sustainable Urban Future*, Council on Tall Buildings and Urban Habitat 8th World Congress, 3–5 March, Dubai, pp23–25

Davey, P. (1997). 'High expectations', in *Architectural Review*, vol. 202, no. 1205, July, pp26–39

Dennis, M. (1986). *Court and Garden*, Boston: The MIT Press

Despommier, D. and Ellingsen, E. (2008). 'The vertical farm: the skyscraper as vehicle for a sustainable urban agriculture', in *Congress Proceedings, Tall and Green: Typology for a Sustainable Urban Future*, Council on Tall Buildings and Urban Habitat 8th World Congress, 3–5 March, Dubai, pp311–317

Dirzo, R. and Mendoza, E. (2008). 'Biodiversity', in *Encyclopedia of Ecology*, eds Jorgensen, S.E. and Fath, B., Amsterdam: Elsevier BV, pp368–377

Evans, G.W. (2003). 'The built environment and mental health', in *Journal of Urban Health*, vol. 80, no. 4, pp536–555

Frampton, K. (1992). *Modern Architecture: A Critical History*, London: Thames & Hudson

Field, B.G. (1992). 'Public space in private development' in *Public Space: Design, Use and Management*, eds Chua, B.H. and Edwards, N., Singapore: Singapore University Press, pp104–114

Gabay, R. and Aravot, I. (2003). 'Using space syntax to understand multi-layer, high-density urban environments', in Proceedings, *4th International Space Syntax Symposium*, London, pp73.1–18

Geist, G.F. (1983). *Arcades: A History of a Building Type*, Boston: The MIT Press

Gotze, H. (1988). 'Roof planting from a constructional viewpoint', in *Garten und Landschaft*, vol. 98, no. 10, pp49–51

Habermas, J. (German (1962) English translation (1989) Thomas Burger). *The Structural Transformation of the Public Sphere: An Inquiry into a Category of Bourgeois Society*, Boston: The MIT Press

Haemmerle, F. (2002). *Der Markt für grüne Dächer wächst immer weiter*, Jahrbuch Dachbegrünung, 2002, pp11–13

Hall, P. (2002). *Cities of Tomorrow*, London: Blackwell

Hillier, B. and Hanson, J. (1984). *The Social Logic of Space*, Cambridge: Cambridge University Press

Hillier, B. and Hanson, J. (1987). 'The architecture of community: some new proposals on the social consequences of architectural and planning decisions', in *Architecture and Behaviour*, vol. 3, no. 3, pp249–273

Hui, S.C.M. and Chan, K.L. (2011). 'Biodiversity assessment of green roofs for green building design' in *Proceedings of Joint Symposium 2011: Integrated Building Design in the New Era of Sustainability*, 22 November 2011, Kowloon, Hong Kong, pp10.1–10.8

Jencks, C. (2002). *The New Paradigm in Architecture: The Language of Post-Modernism*, New Haven, CT: Yale University Press

Johnston, J. and Newton, J. (2004). *Building Green: A Guide to Using Plants on Roofs, Walls and Pavements*, London: Greater London Authority

Jusuf, S.K., Wong, N.H., Hagen, E., Anggoro, R. and Hong, Y. (2007). 'The influence of land use on the urban heat island in Singapore', in *Habitat International*, vol. 31, no. 2, June, pp232–242

Kaiser, H. (1981). 'An attempt at low-cost roof planting', in *Garten und Landschaft*, vol. 91, no. 1, pp30–33

Kaplan, S. (1995). 'The restorative benefits of nature: toward an integrative framework', in *Journal of Environmental Psychology*, issue 15, pp169–182

Kohn, M. (2004). *Brave New Neighborhoods: The Privatization of Public Space*, Routledge: New York

Kuo, F.E., Sullivan, W.C., Coley, R.L. and Brunson, L. (1998). 'Fertile ground for community: inner-city neighborhood common spaces', in *American Journal of Community Psychology*, vol. 26, no. 6, pp823–851

Lozano, E. (1990). *Community Design and the Culture of Cities*, Cambridge: Cambridge University Press

McMillan, D.W. and Chavis, D.M. (1986). 'Sense of community: a definition and theory', in *American Journal of Community Psychology*, vol. 14, no. 1, pp6–23

Madanipour, A. (1998) 'Social exclusion in European cities: processes, experiences and responses', in *The City Reader*, eds LeGates, R.T and Stout, F., London: Routledge, pp181–188

Martin, L. and March, L. (1972) (gen eds). *Urban Space and Structures*, Cambridge: Cambridge University Press

Mason, R.B. (1995). *Muqarnas: Annual on Islamic Art and Architecture*, Leiden: Brill Academic Publishers

Mawhinney, M. (2002). *Sustainable Development: Understanding the Green Debates*, Hoboken, NJ: John Wiley & Sons

Melet, E. and Vreedenburgh, E. (2005). *Rooftop Architecture*, Rotterdam: NAI Publishers

Moore, E.O. (1982). 'A prison environment's effect of health care service demands', in *Journal of Environmental Systems*, vol. 11, no. 1, pp17–34

National Library Board of Singapore (2008). *Redefining the Library*, Singapore: NLB

Newman, O. (1972). *Defensible Space: Crime Prevention through Urban Design*, New York: Macmillan

Newman, O. (1980). *Community of Interest*, Garden City, New York: Anchor/Doubleday

Ng, E. (2010). 'Preface', in *Designing High-Density Cities for Social and Environmental Sustainability*, ed. Ng, E, London: Earthscan, pp xxxi–xxxv

OECD (2012). *Compact City Policies: A Comparative Assessment*, OECD, France

Oldfield, P., Trabucco, D. and Wood, A. (2008). 'Five energy generations of tall buildings: a historical analysis of energy consumption in high rise buildings', in *Congress Proceedings, Tall and Green: Typology for a Sustainable Urban Future*, Council on Tall Buildings and Urban Habitat 8th World Congress, 3–5 March, Dubai, pp 300–310

Ong, B.L. (2003). 'Green plot ratio: an ecological measure for architecture and urban planning', in *Landscape and Urban Planning*, vol. 63, no. 4, May, pp197–210

Osmundson, T. (1999). *Roof Gardens: History, Design and Construction*, New York: WW Norton

Peck, S., Callaghan, C., Kuhn, M. and Bass, B. (1999). *Greenbacks from green roofs: forging a new industry*, Canada: Canada Mortgage and Housing Corporation

Peponis, J., Hadjinikolaou, E.(1989). 'The Spatial Core of Urban Culture', in *Ekistics*, no. 1 pp334-335

Per, A.F., Mozas, J. and Arpa, J. (2011). *This is Hybrid*, Vitoria-Gasteiz: A+T Architecture Publishers

Petersen, A. (1999). *Dictionary of Islamic Architecture*, New York: Routledge

Pomeroy, J. (2005). 'The skycourt as the new square: a thesis on alternative civic spaces for the 21st century', unpublished M. St. thesis, University of Cambridge

Pomeroy, J. (2007). 'The skycourt a viable alternative civic space for the 21st century?', in *CTBUH Journal*, no. 3, pp14–19

Pomeroy, J. (2008). 'Skycourts as transitional space: using space syntax as a predictive theory', in *Congress Proceedings, Tall and Green: Typology for a Sustainable Urban Future*, Council on Tall Buildings and Urban Habitat 8th World Congress, 3–5 March, Dubai, pp580–587

Pomeroy, J. (2009). 'The skycourt a comparison of 4 case studies', in *CTBUH Journal*, no. 1, pp28–36

Pomeroy, J. (2011). 'High density living in the Asian context', in *Journal of Urban Regeneration and Renewal*, vol. 4, no. 4, pp337-349

Pomeroy, J. (2012). 'Greening the urban habitat: Singapore', in *CTBUH Journal*, no. 1, pp30–35

Pomeroy, J. (2012). 'Room at the Top - The Roof as an Alternative Habitable / Social Space in the Singapore Context', in *Journal of Urban Design*, vol. 17, no. 3, pp413-424

Pusharev, B. and Zupan, J. (1975). *Urban Space for Pedestrians*, Boston: The MIT Press

Puteri, S.J. and Ip, K. (2006). 'Linking bioclimatic theory and environmental performance in its climatic and cultural context: an analysis into the tropical highrises of Ken Yeang', in *PLEA 2006, 23rd Conference on Passive and Low Energy Architecture*, Geneva, Switzerland, 6–8 September 2006

Redlich, C.A., Sparer, J. and Cullen, M.R. (1997). 'Sick Building Syndrome', in *The Lancet*, vol. 349, no. 9057, pp1013–1016

Rizwan, A.M., Dennis, L.Y.C. and Liu, C. (2008). 'A review on the generation, determination and mitigation of Urban Heat Island', in *Journal of Environmental Sciences*, vol. 20, no. 1, pp120–128

Roaf, S. (2010). 'The sustainability of high density' in *Designing High-Density Cities for Social and Environmental Sustainability*, ed. Ng, E., London: Earthscan, pp27–39

Roaf, S., Crichton, D. and Nicol, F. (2009). *Adapting Buildings and Cities for Climate Change: A 21st Century Survival Guide*, London: Architectural Press

Rowe, C. and Koetter, F. (1978). *Collage City*, Boston: The MIT Press

Rowe, P.G. (1997). *Civic Realism*, Boston: The MIT Press

Ryan, C.M. and Morrow, L.A. (1992). 'Dysfunctional buildings or dysfunctional people: an examination of the sick building syndrome and allied disorders', in *Journal of Consulting and Clinical Psychology*, vol. 60, no. 2, pp220–240

Sennett, R. (1976). *The Fall of Public Man*, London: Faber & Faber

Shibata, S. and Suzuki, N. (2002). 'Effects of the foliage plant on task performance and mood', in *Journal of Environmental Psychology*, vol. 22, no. 3, pp265–272

Siksna, A. (1998). 'City centre blocks and their evolution: a comparative study of 8 American and Australian CBDs', in *Journal of Urban Design*, vol. 3, no. 3, pp253–284

Sinn, E. (1987). 'Kowloon walled city: its origin and early history', in *Journal of the Hong Kong Branch of the Royal Asiatic Society*, vol. 27, pp30–31

Sudjic, D. (2005). *The Edifice Complex*, London: Penguin

Sukkel, W., Hommes, M. (2009). *Research on agriculture in the Netherlands. Organisation, methodology and results*, Wageningen University, and Louis Bolk Institute

Tauranac, J. (1997). *Empire State: The Making of a Landmark*, New York: St Martins Griffin

Tomlinson, J. (1999). *Globalisation and culture*, Cambridge: Polity press

Tremewan, C. (1994). *The Political Economy of Social Control in Singapore*, London: Macmillan

Ulrich, R.S. (1981). 'Nature versus urban scenes: some psycho-physiological effects', in *Environment and Behavior*, vol. 13, no. 5, pp523–556

Ulrich, R.S. (1983). 'Aesthetic and affective response to the natural environment', in *Human Behaviour and Environment: Advances in Theory and Research*, eds Altman, I. and Wohlwill, J.F., New York: Plenum, pp85–125

Ulrich, R.S. (1986). 'Human responses to vegetation and landscapes', in *Landscape and Urban Planning*, vol. 13, no.1, pp29–44

Ulrich, R.S., Simons, R.F., Losito, B.D., Fiorito, E., Miles., M.A. and Zelson, M. (1990). 'Stress recovery during exposure to natural and urban environments', in *Journal of Environmental Psychology*, vol. 11, no. 3, pp201–230

UNFPA (2007). *State of World Population 2007: Unleashing the Potential for Urban Growth*, New York: UNFPA

URA (2008). *Government Circular on Communal Landscaped Terraces, Sky Terraces and Roof Terraces*, Singapore: Urban Redevelopment Authority

Vollers, K. (2009). 'The CAD-tool 2.0 morphological scheme of non-orthogonal high rises', in *CTBUH Journal*, no. 3, pp38–49

Watkin, D. (2005). *A History of Western Architecture*, New York: Watson-Guptill Publications

Watts, S. (2010). 'The economics of high-rise', in *CTBUH Journal*, no. 3, pp44–45

Webb, M. (1990). *The City Square*, London: Thames & Hudson

Wong, N.H. and Chen, Y. (2006). 'The urban heat island effect in Singapore', in *Tropical Sustainable Architecture: Socio-Environmental Dimensions*, eds Ong, B.L. and Bay, J.H., London: Architectural Press, pp 181–200

Wong, N.H., Wong, V.I., Chen, Y., Soh, J., Ong, C.I. and Sia, A. (2003). 'The effects of a rooftop garden on energy consumption of a commercial building in Singapore', in *Energy and Buildings*, vol. 4, no. 35, pp353–364

Wong, N.H., Tan, A.Y.K., Tan, P.Y. and Wong, N.C. (2009). 'Energy simulations of vertical greenery systems', in *Energy and Building*, vol. 12, no. 41, pp1401–1408

Wong, N.H., Tan, A.Y.K., Tan, P.Y., Chiang, K. and Wong, N.C. (2010). 'Acoustics evaluation of vertical greenery systems for building walls', in *Building and Environment*, vol. 45, no. 2, pp 411–420

Wood, A. (2003). 'Pavements in the sky: use of the skybridge in tall buildings', in *Architectural Research Quarterly (ARQ)*, vol. 7, no. 3/4, pp325–333

Wood, A. (2009). 'Singapore visit, August 2009', in *CTBUH Journal*, no. 3, pp52–56

World Commission on Environment and Development (Brundtland report)(1987). *Our Common Future*, Oxford: Oxford University Press

Yeang, K. (2002). *Reinventing the Skyscraper*, Hoboken, NJ: Wiley Academic

Zimrig, C. (1983). 'The built environment as a source of psychological stress: impacts of buildings and cities on satisfaction and behaviour' in *Environmental Stress*, ed. Evans, G.W., Cambridge: Cambridge University Press, pp151–178

Zukin, S. (1996). *The Cultures of Cities*, London: Blackwell

Zukin, S. (2011). *Naked City: The Death and Life of Authentic Urban Places*, Oxford: Oxford University Press

Index

References in *italics* indicate figures

#

20 Fenchurch Street, London 126, *127–9*
45-degree line 69, *69*, *71*

A

Abeno HARUKAS, Osaka 146, *147–9*
Abu Dhabi: Sikkas in the Sky (design) 260, *260*;
    Solar Parking (design) 272, *272*
Academy of Sciences, California *258*
accessibility suffocation 48
acoustic buffers 53, *55*
Acqua Livingstone, Manila *247*
ACROS Fukuoka Prefectural International Hall *52*,
    84, *85–7*
Adrian Smith + Gordon Gill 188, *189–91*
agriculture, urban *see* urban agriculture
air rights *64*, 270–2, *270*, *273*; *see also* One
    Madison Avenue, New York
Al-Fustat, Egypt 36
Allen Lambert Galleria, Toronto 52
Angkasa Raya, Kuala Lumpur 172, *173–5*
aquaponic systems 276
arcades 31, *31*, 52
Asia: tall buildings 25
Atelier Hollein 180, *181–3*
atria: benefits of 52; full height 37, 80, *83*, 88, *89*,
    91, 92, *95*
attention restoration theory *56–7*
Australia: One Central Park, Sydney 138, *139–41*

B

Babylon, Hanging Gardens of 36
balance theory of sustainability 256
Ballard, JG 27
Bangkok: Red Sky *65*
Banham, Rayner 52, 246, 247
Barcelona: Urban Projects Programme 17, *17*
Bay, Joo Hwa 57–8
Bedok Court, Singapore 57–8, *58*
Behnisch Architekten 92, *93–5*
Beijing: Galaxy SOHO 100, *101–3*; Linked Hybrid
    42, *42*, 104, *105–7*
Beirut Terraces, Lebanon 154, *155–7*
best practice recommendations 68

Betsky, Aaron 68
betterment levy 32
bio-diversity 60–2, *62*, *63*, 84, 138
Biopolis, Singapore *245*
Bjarke Ingels Group 168, *169–71*
Blue Cross Blue Shield Tower, Chicago *271*
Boeri Studio 118, *119–21*
Bosco Verticale, Milan 118, *119–21*
brown roofs 60, *63*
Brundtland Report 256
Büro Ole Scheeren 172, *173–5*

C

Campo, Siena 16, *16*
Canada: Allen Lambert Galleria, Toronto *52*;
    Ontario College of Art and Design, Toronto *64*
capitalism 18–19
carbon dioxide 53
car parking, vertical 272, *272*
Charles Correa Associates 76, *77–9*
Cheng, Vicky 40
Chicago: Blue Cross Blue Shield Tower *271*; City
    Hall 68, *68*; green roofs 68
China: Fake Hills, Beihai 142, *143–5*;
    Galaxy SOHO, Beijing 100, *101–3*;
    Linked Hybrid, Beijing 42, *42*, 104, *105–7*;
    SBF Tower, Shenzhen 180, *181–3*;
    Shanghai Tower 130, *131–3*;
    Vertical Farmland, Shanghai (design) 226, *227–9*;
    World Financial Centre, Shanghai *263*; *see
    also* Hong Kong
Ciliwung Recovery Programme (CRP) 234
circulation 48–50, *48–51*, *103*, 245, 266–8, *266–9*;
    see also skybridges
City Hall, Chicago 68, *68*
city of objects 23–5, *26–9*, 259–60
city of spaces 22–3, 26, 259–60
civility 15, 18
Clarke Quay, Singapore *258*
Columbia University Medical Center, New York
    196, *197–9*
Commerzbank, Frankfurt 37–8, *39*, 88,
89–91

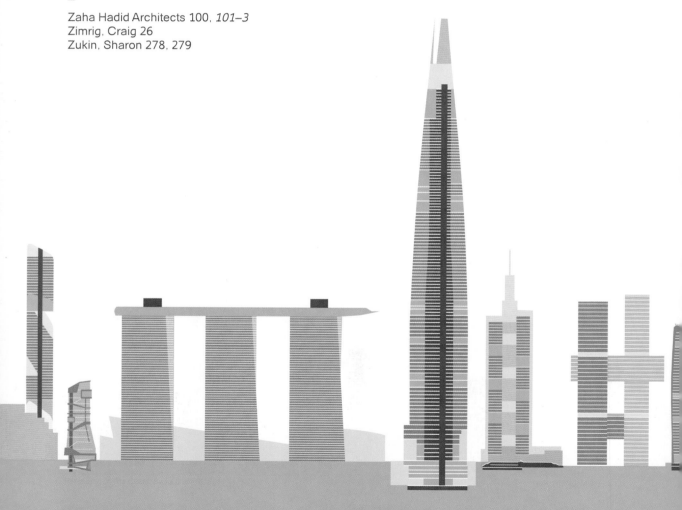

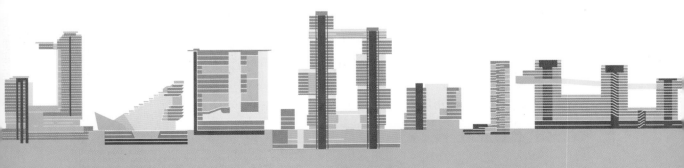

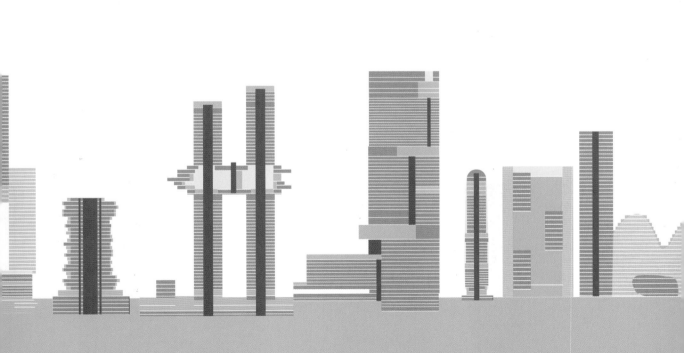